Praise for Paul A. Laudicina

"Paul, I've had the distinct privilege of knowing you for most of your professional lifetime . . . You have always had a remarkable ability to translate complicated policy questions into clear and compelling propositions that average Americans can understand."

—Joe Biden

Praise for *Roadmap to a Brighter Future*

"This sensible, powerful, and supremely practical book is a welcome prescription to help us navigate out of the maze of political discord and bitterness in which America finds itself today."

—Admiral James Stavridis, US Navy (Ret); former Dean,
Fletcher School of Law and Diplomacy, Tufts University;
former NATO Supreme Allied Commander Europe

"Paul A. Laudicina has written a manifesto for America in the coming decade. His energy, vision, and faith in our future shine through the pages and his scenarios for where the country could and should go make for compelling reading."

—Anne-Marie Slaughter, CEO, New America; former Dean,
School of Public and International Affairs, Princeton University

"Paul A. Laudicina is an outstanding thought leader. If you are seeking clarity in a time of uncertainty, and hope in a time of despair, Paul is the author to read."

—Mukesh Ambani, Founder and Chairman, Reliance Industries

"*Roadmap to a Brighter Future* captures the intensity of the hard choices society must make and vividly paints credible scenarios ahead about the fragility of America's purpose at home and abroad. Paul Laudicina tells us how to get it right. But will we listen?"

—Steve Clemons, Editor at Large, *The Hill*

"Drawing on his rich network, strongly anchored in relevant historical examples, and brought to life through meaningful alternative future scenarios for the US, Paul brings much-needed optimism, while reminding us that nothing is predestined and that we must take responsibility for the future we want to see."

—Paul Bulcke, Chairman of the Board, Nestlé

"Few people can match the encyclopedic knowledge that Paul Laudicina has accumulated in his fascinating career. His wisdom and broad experience shine through in this book. There is no better thoughtful guide for managing through these challenging times than this volume."

—Kishore Mahbubani, founding Dean, Lee Kuan Yew School of Public Policy, National University of Singapore; Author of *Has China Won?*

"Few authors have the insightfulness, incisiveness and intelligence to bridge the pragmatic and the profound like Paul Laudicina. He not only discerns the divisions we face today, he manages to challenge us as leaders, and as a country, to see our more integrative and enduring potential. Beyond a brilliant read, this book is a mindset and heartset shifting experience for us all."

—Kevin Cashman, Global Co-Leader of CEO and Enterprise Leader Development, Korn Ferry; Author of *Leadership from the Inside Out* and *The Pause Principle*

"*Roadmap* provides bold and practical prescriptions for how the country can draw on its history of momentous transformation and once again renew itself as a stronger and better and more inclusive society."

—Richard Florida, Author of *The Rise of the Creative Class*

"This book is a must read for anyone interested in the future of the world. Every CEO should read it!"

—Sebastian Edwards, Henry Ford II Professor, UCLA Anderson School of Management; Author of *American Default*

"From a longtime friend and former staffer of Joe Biden's, Paul Laudicina's book could not land at a more opportune time. Laudicina gives America a clear and much needed way ahead for a country whose best days could still lie ahead—if it would only pay heed to the wise counsel of those such as Laudicina. The time is fully ripe for Laudicina's excellently-argued roadmap."

—Edward Luce, US National Editor, *Financial Times*

"Amid all its current problems, America is disheartened, confused, and lacking in confidence. Paul Laudicina shows a pathway back to full vigor and economic hope. This book is refreshing, enjoyable, and above all a beautiful mixture of practicality and inspiration. Wonderful, and badly needed at this time!"

—W. Brian Arthur, Economist, Santa Fe Institute; Visiting Researcher, Intelligent Systems Lab, PARC

"The future belongs to realistic optimists, and Paul Laudicina articulates this beautifully and why this is so true for the US today. It should be read by all business, political, and civil society leaders, maybe twice!"

—Muhtar Kent, former Chairman & CEO, The Coca-Cola Company; Board Member, Special Olympics

"In this penetrating and lively book, Paul Laudicina notes there are many possible futures. But, above all, it provides a vision of the better future we ought to choose. We must put our trust, not in unreasoning fear, but in rational hope. This book provides just that."

—Martin Wolf CBE, Chief Economics Commentator, *Financial Times*

"Don't bet against progress, Paul Laudicina advises in this insightful, heartfelt, and sizzlingly written book."

—Edward Lucas, Columnist, *The Times*; former Senior Editor, *The Economist*

"Paul Laudicina's book is the strong dose of optimism and rationality we desperately need. A must read for policy makers, business executives . . . and everyone who cares about uplifting humanity."

—Vivek Wadhwa, Distinguished Fellow, Labor and Worklife Program, Harvard Law School

"History, sociology, and economics are woven together in a breezy readable style to structure this volume on the challenges facing America but also the outlines for a brighter future."

—Catherine Mann, former Global Chief Economist, Citibank; former Chief Economist and G20 Finance Deputy, OECD

"Read this compelling think piece to peer into America's promising future and how to 'get our mojo back.'"

—Josef Joffe, Professor of Practice, Johns Hopkins University; Distinguished Visiting Fellow, Stanford University.

"Paul's brutally honest and equally insightful views on the past, present and future are a must read!"

—Mpumi Madisa, CEO, Bidvest Group

"Paul Laudicina has always brought an exceptionally perceptive eye and superb judgement to his analysis of the world's problems. Read what he has to say. It matters, and he has valuable insights for all of us."

—Sir Rod Eddington AO, former CEO, British Airways and Cathay Pacific Airways

"Paul Laudicina offers an encouraging multi-faceted view on how to get on a much better track to the future. Although focused on America, it is a must read for the entire world as we are all facing the described transformational changes!"

—Jürgen Hambrecht, Supervisory Board Member, Daimler AG; former Chairman, BASF

ROADMAP
TO A
BRIGHTER
FUTURE

Also by Paul A. Laudicina

*Beating the Global Odds: Successful Decision-making
in a Confused and Troubled World*

*World Out of Balance: Navigating Global Risks
to Seize Competitive Advantage*

ROADMAP
TO A
BRIGHTER
FUTURE

REIMAGINING AND REALIZING
AMERICA'S POSSIBILITIES

PAUL A. LAUDICINA

Matt Holt Books
An Imprint of BenBella Books, Inc.
Dallas, TX

BenBella Books, Inc.
10440 N. Central Expressway
Suite 800
Dallas, TX 75231
benbellabooks.com
Send feedback to feedback@benbellabooks.com

BenBella is a federally registered trademark
Matt Holt and logo are trademarks of BenBella Books

Printed in the United States of America
10 9 8 7 6 5 4 3 2 1

Library of Congress Control Number: 2021012410
ISBN 9781953295644 (print)
ISBN 9781953295989 (ebook)

Copyediting by James Fraleigh
Proofreading by Greg Teague and Dylan Julian
Indexing by WordCo Indexing Services
Text design and composition by PerfecType, Nashville, TN
Cover design by Brigid Pearson
Printed by Lake Book Manufacturing

To my children, grandchildren, and their generations, whose future will be shaped by the critical decisions we make today

CONTENTS

PREFACE

This book is all about architecting the future we want by understanding more clearly the alternative futures that lie ahead of us, how the optimal ones among them can best be realized, and how the more dangerous ones can be avoided. The *Sturm und Drang* of the late Trump presidency and the early COVID-19 era seemed like an especially propitious time to employ the navigational tools this volume advocates to chart a "roadmap to a brighter future." Along with the untold pain and suffering of the novel coronavirus pandemic came many unexpected things—substantial blocks of time for reflection among them. It is out of that involuntary pause that this book emerged.

To most, the notion of trying to foresee the future in periods of extreme volatility and uncertainty is a fool's errand. Yet it is precisely in the midst of the fog of ambiguity that one needs to find some sense of direction toward a desired destination. Of course, once the fog lifts, it takes little clairvoyance or courage to follow the path to one's desired destination. Even so, as the ink was drying on the final page of this narrative, the world was still gripped by great uncertainty and anxiety, despite increasing signs of hope on the horizon.

The pandemic-imposed isolation not only facilitated self-reflection, but also—ironically—enabled social connection as we found new pathways to engage others. I was one of those fortunate ones who not only had the resources to live comfortably in relative isolation while too many others suffered, but also had the option to stay purposefully and passionately engaged with family, friends, and colleagues despite the mayhem in the world just beyond my front door (and mask).

In these pages I will share with the reader a series of recommendations, some of which have been espoused by the Biden administration but were crafted before Joe Biden was elected. So it will come as no surprise that I have been a Joe Biden enthusiast for the more than four decades I have had the privilege to know and work with the man who is now the 46th president of the United States. And I became convinced early on in his pursuit of the presidency that he was the absolute right man for this especially challenging period of history. I believe this will be increasingly apparent to all as they observe how Joe Biden's special blend of experience, judgment, humility, empathy, passion, and purpose are applied to digging us out of the very deep and dark hole we were in when he took office.

Nonetheless, the alternative futures I outline in these pages do not assume that an especially bright future is inevitable. Rather, that future will be realized only if we are smart enough to envision it and courageous enough to enable it. That is precisely what I hope this book will do: jumpstart your imagination to envision the possibilities that lie within our reach, ignite your optimism to believe those possibilities are achievable, and galvanize your resolve to pursue them—knowing that failure to do so will likely result in an unacceptably bad alternative future.

"Challenges" is a catch-all euphemism these days intended to capture the cascading crises that have shaken the very foundations of societies across a broad swath of geographies, cultures, and demographics. This book will trace the fault lines running just below the surface of these seemingly unconnected realities in an attempt to better understand why we appear to be so mired in social discord, unable to move forward with common cause in the common interest. But, as we all know, though diagnosing the malady is necessary, diagnosis is not a cure.

Unlike many other contemporary volumes, *Roadmap to a Brighter Future* is not content to stop at admiring the fire—that is, taking the view of a passive bystander. Rather, my ambition for readers of this book is that they will come away understanding where we are and why we are there, while appreciating that we have been in equally or even more difficult straits before. In the words of the late poet laureate Maya Angelou: "How do you know where you're going if you don't know where you've been?" At the same time, my hope is that this book will not only help readers powerfully imagine brighter alternative futures, but also equip them with the prescriptive propositions that need to be employed to realize that future.

But in today's "breathe your own exhaust" world of alternate realities, finding consensus around any proposed destination is tough. If you don't trust the map you're reading (or, as my kids are more likely to say, the GPS you're following), and you don't even trust the navigator's ability or intention, then you can hardly get to where you need to go, or expect anyone to go along with you. So the task of restoring what has been for much of our history a quintessentially American pragmatic optimism will be neither easy nor quick. We begin that process in the pages of this book by digging through the layers of sediment that have obscured our vision, sapped our confidence, and diverted us from addressing chronic and fundamental problems at the center of today's crisis in confidence.

To repeat what should by now be painfully obvious to most, Donald Trump was not the cause of our ills, though he surely exacerbated them in many devastatingly pernicious ways. Rather, we as a nation—along with many others around the world—have been on this slippery, downward slope for the last few decades. While elites were cashing in on the fruits of technologically-induced, policy-liberalized global integration, much of the rest of the world was barely getting by, and actually falling further behind. And this divide, both within and between countries, was

low-hanging fruit for populist demagogues and their loyal followers prepared to carry out their will no matter what. So restoring trust in our
systems of governance, and in the commitment and ability of our leaders
to restore the accessibility of the American Dream, will take time. Getting the buy-in across various national divides needed to implement the
propositions advocated in this book, however practical and logical they
are, will take skill and hard work. Anyone expecting a quick turnaround
is delusional. As Thomas Edison reminded us, "vision without execution
is hallucination."

I thank you for joining me on the journey outlined in these pages. I
hope you will find the reasoning compelling, the vision uplifting, and the
propositions necessary to reimagine and realize that vision of a brighter
future irresistible.

—PAL

January 20, 2021

INTRODUCTION

THERE IS ONE PAST, AND ONE PRESENT, BUT MULTIPLE POSSIBLE FUTURES

"Vision is the art of seeing
what is invisible to others."
—JONATHAN SWIFT

History will record 2020 as an *annus horribilis* for the United States, during which we were literally plagued by a deadly virus that overwhelmed the world within months, followed by the worst economic dislocation since the Great Depression; racial tensions that flared up across the country; unrelenting severe weather across its expanse; and a brutal, scorched-earth presidential election and tortured transfer of power that left many Americans feeling more angry, confused, and divided than ever.

Then, 2021 launched with both hope and continued peril: promising vaccine developments, after overcoming initial logistical challenges; and historic and optimistic Senate elections in Georgia, marred the day they were decided by an angry mob storming our nation's Capitol in an attempt to thwart congressional certification of a clear electoral mandate.

Despite this turmoil, we are not predestined to live in such a dystopian, broken, or badly functioning society. Yet a better version of the future won't emerge spontaneously—which is why I am writing this

1

book. We can overcome these and other profound problems, as we've done in past times of crisis and turmoil, and emerge stronger. This book is about how we can do just that. But first we'll need to make sense of what hit us, where we are now, and how we can move forward.

To many, the COVID-19 pandemic felt like the last straw in an already deeply unsettled and polarized world, forcing changes we could barely have envisioned, much less understand. Whether we like it or not, we now live in a world transformed. Many of the "preexisting conditions" that were in the background before COVID-19 have been advanced and greatly amplified. It's no exaggeration to say we are living through the most complex and challenging period in our lifetimes—possibly in modern history. No wonder the public is severely disoriented while many of their leaders look for a playbook.

Like a tide rolling out to expose the vestiges of shipwrecks, the pandemic revealed our nation's weaknesses and fault lines (and, more rarely, its strengths). Some of these vulnerabilities were already evident in our societies, governments, companies, and institutions of all kinds; others heaved just below the surface.

Surely many casualties of the seemingly cruel reckoning of the pandemic could have been avoided with more capable leadership and a public that demanded better solutions to the problems COVID-19 posed and more transparent and accountable leadership. The quality of leadership was the not-so-secret sauce shaping the reputations and fortunes of countries, governments, companies, and their leaders as they went through this crucible. As in the scene on any battlefield when the smoke of engagement lifts, the sight was ghastly, and the war is not over yet, even as increasingly we see the virus itself through the rearview mirror in much of the world.

Young, high-flying Singaporean government official and poet Aaron Maniam admitted that even our current vocabulary was insufficient to describe what we had been living through. In his TED Talk, Maniam mused that, owing to the gravity of the COVID-19 pandemic, we have been using mostly wartime-style military metaphors—for instance, "defeating the virus"—which helped maintain public order by creating victors and enemies. He suggested we ought to expand our terminology to include such expressions as "journey" or "ecology." For example, we might need to learn to live and function with this pandemic and others for a long time. Further, the pandemic experiences of people worldwide have ranged from mild lockdown sabbaticals to extreme trauma: unevenly distributed, and devastating the poor and underserved far more harshly. Clearly our words have seemed to fail us or feel inadequate in this new territory.

The Malthusian hand also hit some business sectors worse than others. Some of these, like airlines, struggled to stay viable until people felt secure enough to travel again, with passenger numbers picking up. But luring the world back to pre-pandemic behavior won't be uniformly easy, or necessarily even desirable. In one macabre sign of the times, top-tier carrier Emirates not only offered free medical care for any passengers who contracted the coronavirus while flying with them, but also free first-class funerals if they ended up dying—not the most compelling enticement.

But a hard-headed look at the facts—and human history—offers reasonable hope for better days ahead. The future need not be just an endless cascade of crises rendering us this helpless, prompting some to pull radical political levers, check out from positive social connection, or—worse yet—become one of the mounting tally of "deaths of despair," including those lost to suicide or substance abuse. The public, in the US and worldwide, yearns for better times imbued with decency, security, and hope. With the right leadership—and the right new policies—we can and will be able to realize those legitimate, universal expectations. But it will take a change in mindset and behavior, as likely driven—and demanded—from the bottom up as from the top down.

In this book, I will explain what I believe we *concretely and pragmatically* must do to get ourselves on a much better track to the future, in a sustainably resilient way. With such solutions in hand, we'll be able to handle whatever future mega-problems or crises come our way, having learned from our success and failures when we grappled with the consequences of 9/11, the global financial crisis of the late 2000s, and, more recently, the evolving pandemic. As COVID-19 has made all too tragically clear, the stakes are enormous, both for our present and our potential futures. If we're not smart enough to imagine and anticipate possible futures, both desirable and flawed, we surely won't be ready to steer toward better outcomes. We'd do well to recall the Cheshire Cat's advice to a confused Alice when she inquired about where she should go in Wonderland: "That depends a good deal on where you want to get to."

When the Berlin Wall fell more than 30 years ago, we indeed heralded the dawn of opened markets, global integration, spreading prosperity, and seemingly limitless growth, alongside the growing embrace of Western democratic governance, supported and enhanced by technological advances. I vividly recall those heady days in the early 1990s when we launched our Kearney CEO think tank, the Global Business Policy Council, with all the promise of a rapidly integrating world. In hindsight, that unabashedly sunny outlook—seemingly so inevitable, inexorable, and immutable—would extend only so far before centrifugal forces, buried just below the surface of the expansive globalization framework itself, would reemerge.

Instead, most of us have come to accept that our world is one of converging existential threats: dangers to public health, growing wealth disparities, rampant populism and protectionist practices, civil and racial unrest, geopolitical instability, and the devastating impact of severe weather induced by climate change. Not to mention nonstop technological innovations that simultaneously dazzle and appropriately scare us, like artificial intelligence (AI). By the way, when I speak of "existential threats" facing America (and the world), I don't always mean that they necessarily threaten the very *existence* of the United States, but rather that they put at grave risk both the best attributes of America as we have known them and our still high hopes for our nation in the future.

We have the power to destroy ourselves more quickly and completely than ever before, or to purposefully create a future filled with greater opportunity and justifiable promise and optimism. But we must first begin with a sober, brutally honest assessment of what will get us from here to there. Leadership coach Marshall Goldsmith's notion about how one does that as an individual could well be applied more broadly to ushering in that more positive future: "What got you here won't get you there."

Of all the converging existential threats we face, I am optimistic about how America can and will address four in particular: public health, economic growth, climate change, and racial justice.

Why am I optimistic? Simply put, I believe (1) we are not now, and never have been, mere hostages to forces beyond our control; (2) a different trajectory and better outcomes are more possible today than ever; and (3) leadership still matters—enormously, in fact—and can help midwife that better future. And we already see the difference that effective, purposeful, and principled leadership can make, as the Biden administration has set its sights on taking action to address all four of the aforementioned threats—much as was promised during the 2020 campaign—and is already showing progress on what is clearly a long-term agenda.

As noted Stanford scholar and thinker Francis Fukuyama, of *End of History* fame, tells us, times of crisis tend to catapult societies—and indeed the world—in new directions. That's why it is so much better to shape the future than to be on the receiving end of seemingly uncontrollable forces that shape it for us.

As Frank put it in a 2020 *Foreign Affairs* article, "Major crises have major consequences, usually unforeseen. The Great Depression spurred isolationism, nationalism, fascism, and World War II—but also led to the New Deal, the rise of the United States as a global superpower, and eventually decolonization. The 9/11 attacks produced two failed American interventions, the rise of Iran, and new forms of Islamic radicalism. The 2008 financial crisis generated a surge in anti-establishment populism that replaced leaders across the globe."

Few doubt that the pandemic acted as a fast-forward button, whisking us into the future whether we were ready or not. As the saying goes, even a stopped clock is right twice a day, and so, too, even a monster of history like Lenin could be correct in supposedly having said, "There are decades where nothing happens; and there are weeks when decades happen." That certainly seems to have been our recent experience. When I spoke with Mayo Clinic CEO Dr. Gianrico Farrugia during the height of the pandemic, he acknowledged the obvious challenges but also noted that even terrible crises can have an upside if we learn and innovate as a result. In Gianrico's view, "The pandemic has been a catalyst . . . it's been an accelerator."

Urbanist Richard Florida, who you'll be hearing more about later in the book, sees upside in the remote-working revolution accelerated by the pandemic, as people are able to work from less costly and more enjoyable locations. As he wrote in 2021: "Smaller metro areas such as Miami, Austin, Charlotte, Nashville and Denver enjoy a price advantage over more expensive cities like New York and San Francisco, and they are using it to attract newly mobile professionals. Smaller cities like Gilbert, Ariz., Boulder, Colo., Bentonville, Ark., and Tulsa, Okla., have joined the competition as well, some of them launching initiatives specifically designed to appeal to remote workers. And more rural communities including Bozeman, Mont., Jackson Hole, Wyo., Truckee, Calif., and New York's Hudson Valley are becoming the nation's new 'Zoom towns,' seeing their fortunes rise from the influx of new residents whose work relies on such digital tools."

Even more bullish about the period ahead is Dutch historian Rutger Bregman, author of several bestsellers including *Utopia for Realists*, who believes we've long overstated the nasty side of human nature, thanks to influential philosophers like Machiavelli and Hobbes. In Bregman's view, science shows we're actually hardwired for cooperation and more inclined to trust one another than we think—a very good thing, given how recent crises have overlapped. According to Bregman, "human generosity isn't merely optimistic—it's realistic." I think he's got a point, and we're certainly going to need a lot of new cooperation and solidarity of all kinds, at all levels, to solve our current problems and prepare for whatever hits us next. America has always been noted for its optimism in the face of every challenge—perhaps not surprising for a melting pot of peoples from differing backgrounds sharing one common denominator: the intention and determination to seize opportunities and create a better life. And Americans have had a shared dedication to the values upon which our country was founded, even if they've been dramatically tested in recent times.

Transformational leaders are able to catalyze that generosity of spirit and optimism by offering an uplifting vision of the future and convincing followers that such a favorable change in direction is achievable. But even the most inspirational and aspirational vision will require leaders advocating that vision to be seen as authentically capable of delivering it fairly and equitably. It was the authenticity and optimism of then-candidate Joe Biden's message, along with voters' belief in his experience-based credibility for delivering on a new, unifying vision for America, that led them—in the midst of 2020's mayhem—to elect him with the largest tally in US history.

So, however big the "megatrends" coming our way, or the odds we may appear to be up against, we need not be passive recipients of unacceptable outcomes. The future isn't a fate to which we're sentenced. Rather, the future is a *choice* we can and must help determine.

But first we need to envision the future we want, and then act with resolve and determination to *will* into being the specific outcomes we want for ourselves and future generations. "More of the same" and "business as usual" won't cut it, nor will more kicking the can down the road. Yale Law School professor Daniel Markovits has called our tendency to try to find low-budget remedies for profound problems "cheap cures for deep ills." Enough is enough. So let's return to our quintessentially American pragmatic approach to problem-solving and create a better future. We can't afford not to. The stakes are enormous. We'll either get this right, and we'll all benefit—or we won't, and we will all lose.

PART 1

WHERE ARE WE AND HOW DID WE GET HERE?

We all know the last couple of years have been rough. Many experienced their first catastrophic personal and economic losses; others have felt such pain for decades. In fact, for many Americans, the pandemic was just another agonizing moment after years of increasing struggle.

I know the last thing anyone wants right now is more negativity, but I do think that taking an honest, holistic look at reality is the only way we'll be able to learn from today's challenges and grow. In these next two chapters, I'm not going to hold back: it's been tough out there, and we all need to understand what has changed, what remains the same, and the implications of both. However, I do not for one second believe that we need to resign ourselves to one or another unfortunate future.

CHAPTER ONE

America had already been contending with four existential threats: public health, inequality and economic dislocation, racial injustice, and climate change . . . and in 2020 they all converged to create a year from hell.

OKAY, WE'VE BEEN LIVING IN A DISASTER MOVIE. HOW DO WE BRING IT TO A POSITIVE END?

"In crises the most daring course is often the safest."
—HENRY KISSINGER

"Success is not final; failure is not fatal: it is the courage to continue that counts."
—*ATTRIBUTED TO* SIR WINSTON CHURCHILL

We didn't need a global public health crisis like the pandemic to realize we have been living through a time of great upheaval. This dizzying swirl of challenges includes a rising, muscle-flexing China, a troublemaking Russia, the shadow of continuing Islamist-extremist terrorism, Brexit-style political fragmentation, political hucksterism, challenges to democratic institutions and practices, growing gross inequities and endemic racism, extreme weather in every compass direction, and widely divergent understanding and acceptance of objective fact and truth . . . all amid the proliferation of dazzling tech and the lightning-fast spread of both information and disinformation.

Massive wildfires from the Western US to Australia, which blocked out the sun over many major cities, only added to the apocalyptic tone of the recent past and present. What's next, some may ask: A plague of locusts? (As it happens, a locust invasion of what some termed biblical scale hit an already troubled East Africa in 2020.) It's no wonder Twitter users were calling for 2020—a year from hell for so many—to be "canceled," as reflected in the global enthusiasm to celebrate a new year (if in uncharacteristically muted, sheltered-in-place fashion) as the clock struck midnight on December 31, 2020.

However, the start of 2021 brought no immediate relief. Just six days into the new year, the attacks on the US Capitol signaled the continuation of a troubling trend—the rise of homegrown right-wing extremist attacks, which the Center for Strategic and International Studies has found are currently at their highest levels in decades. Alongside this development were plenty of mixed signals: from virus fatigue to vaccine euphoria; from post-Trump political relief to continued partisan wrangling; from a nation yearning to unite to intermittent manifestations of political radicalism. Throughout all the turbulence, the nation has taken on a more hopeful tone.

Yet some parts of America don't share that hopeful note. As Clint Smith, the Black poet and father of two young children, observed, protests in the streets of America over racial justice happened during a global pandemic that was disproportionately killing people of color. And this grim, unequal reality is a function of institutional racism, a history of housing segregation, medical discrimination, low-wage jobs, a stark racial wealth gap, and a lack of access to quality healthcare and education. The pandemic has shone a harsh light on a cruel legacy that is nonetheless awakening the soul of America.

All the while, technological and commercial innovation zooms upward, continuing to enrich the top tiers of societies—"a rising tide lifts all yachts," some have quipped—while leaving many young adults and ordinary people behind. Traditional career paths are uncertain at best, and gone at worst, with steady income and paths to homeownership out of reach for many just starting out or those down on their luck.

The mood in recent years has soured for millions, who regard some cyberpunk version of *Blade Runner* as the default scenario for what the future might look like—a "high tech, low life" surveillance state where ordinary folk live as drones and pass their leisure time consuming entertainment and drugs, both legal and illegal. Of course, China has already implemented an AI-driven surveillance state of such pervasive social control that the nightmares of the sci-fi series *Black Mirror* seem, if anything, increasingly representative of the near, rather than more distant, future.

Precursors of that dystopian science fiction future already exist in some parts of the world. Maybe you've heard of Japan's *hikikomori*? About a million Japanese young people and adults never leave their bedrooms for six months or more at a time, such is their total alienation from the expectations and stresses of life. This disturbing phenomenon also appears to be spreading: in Italy, around a hundred thousand young people between 14 and 25 can also be classified as *hikikomori*, according to the newspaper *La Stampa*, which seems quite countercultural for that highly social Mediterranean country. This is not a mental illness, but a symptom of profound societal distress, a purely voluntary kind of self-isolation and lockdown that started long before COVID-19.

Speaking of Japan, in 2012, Sony Corporation unveiled a set of scenarios for what the world might look like in 2025, called "Sony Future-Scapes." As it happens, one of the four scenarios the Sony brain trust offered was called "Centralized Survival"—a dark vision of a world under great duress, with restrictions on personal freedom put in place to ensure some modicum of order and to keep people alive. I'm sorry to say that parts of that Sony scenario turned out to be uncomfortably prophetic.

In the newer dystopian scenarios that futurists are developing now, various technologies, including AI, will run our daily lives, and the "lucky" ones are presumed to be those living in the West, where at least you'll be able to choose reasonably freely what to spend your days and evenings watching on some future version of Netflix.

Is this the future we really want?

The global pandemic turbocharged this broad-based, almost ontological sense of insecurity, in which an invisible pathogen of lightning speed and indiscriminate universality threatened the most basic human claims to physical, financial, and emotional security—a perfect storm created by severe "weather" conditions on every front.

But what if I told you that, despite how dire things have seemed for so many, a better future for ourselves and our children was well within reach? In one of my four possible visions for the future, *All-American Comeback*, which I describe later in the book, the United States does not just recover from its present-day maladies, but actually succeeds in becoming more equitable, prosperous, and innovative than ever. This is more than wishful thinking. I am convinced that an optimistic vision of the future is indeed achievable. We simply need to marshal our American can-do spirit and inventiveness, with effective leadership pointing the way and enabling the path forward.

As far as the feeling of living in a disaster movie or horror film goes, it's all too easy for some to imagine only the worst from here on out. I believe such a default assumption is wrongheaded; we must not resign ourselves to its seeming inevitability. I surely don't, perhaps because I've lived through my own near–disaster movie and am still here to write this book.

In 1996, during the initial boom of corporate bonding adventures, my wife, daughter, and I traveled to Arizona for a company meeting that featured an "extracurricular" balloon expedition with peers. My early-morning outing would become, later that day, the top national TV news story. Our bad luck began with a balloon pilot who, as we learned later, had mental health and drug problems. Then, the pleasure of sailing above the Sonoran Desert became a nightmare when our balloon descended abruptly and hit the ground hard; our pilot fell out, by the way. Then, as the rest of us re-ascended, the balloon's suspension cables caught fire and smoldered ominously. We first-time ballooners were now headed toward downtown Phoenix with no other safe landing zones in reach, assuming we were able to navigate through a minefield of high-tension power lines . . . all without a pilot. When we finally landed, all remaining twelve of us in the gondola, including myself, were injured, but we did manage to survive this disaster scenario—despite the harrowing conditions and no pilot—by working together and not accepting defeat.

I can assure you that the near-death experience of flying without a pilot in a smoldering hot air balloon focuses one's mind and spirit on what really matters in life. But it has also taught me that we can steer most crises that afflict us toward a good outcome. My fateful balloon accident could have ended tragically had those of us in the basket not worked together with the ground crew via walkie-talkie (in those pre–cell phone days) to land the balloon safely (broken bones and bloody bruises notwithstanding). So even when things are pretty bleak, active, intelligent, purposeful, and courageous engagement can yield a seemingly impossible happy ending.

If we accept that there's a way out of even the gravest circumstances—and I believe there is—then what? First, before we plot our escape, it's important to better understand what got us to where we are today. There are many terms to describe our recent national and global predicament. Perfect storm. Disaster movie. Converging crises. Weariness. Toxic legacies. Again, many things collided to bring us to this unsteady juncture: uneven post–Great Recession growth; the fear of "the other" (sparked by 9/11 but now including migrants and immigrants in general, and, increasingly, AI-turbocharged, job-eroding automation); a diminishing sense of community and social cohesion as people devote an ever-larger slice of their free time to staring into their devices; economic progress that disproportionately benefits "the haves"; racial injustice, bigotry, and discrimination rearing their ugly heads . . . and much more.

Many of us, myself included, have benefited disproportionately from the largesse of a peaceful, globally integrated, and technologically enabled world. But so many others have been left, as it were, outside the bakery window looking in.

Beginning in the 1970s, income growth for middle- and lower-income families in the United States slowed sharply, while income for those of us at the very top of the ladder rose to levels not seen since the Roaring Twenties a century ago (ironically after emerging from the last global pandemic, the "Spanish flu" of 1918–20). These inequities only got worse after the Great Recession of 2007–09, which produced nasty effects that still linger and affect us today. Research from the Economic Policy Institute shows that in 15 of the 24 states they studied, all income growth from 2009–13 went to the richest 1 percent. If you wondered why rallying against the "1 percent" became a cry for economic justice after the Great Recession, there's your answer.

Even today, wealth discrepancies show no sign of narrowing. The bottom 50 percent of earners held $2 trillion in wealth during the second quarter of 2020, the same amount as the top 50 richest Americans. In other words, 50 people combined held the same amount of wealth as 165 million Americans. And the pandemic only made the rich richer: both Elon Musk and Jeff Bezos—two of the world's richest people—saw their net worth grow to more than $180 billion during the first 10 months of the pandemic, far above pre-pandemic levels. Plus, *Forbes* estimates that nearly 500 people became billionaires during the pandemic year, or roughly one per every 17 hours. Meanwhile almost half of American families surveyed reported having "serious financial problems" in September 2020, with one in six forgoing bill payments to buy food. Clearly, something is wrong with this picture. This inequity helps explain why calls during the 2020 election to increase taxes on the country's wealthiest, including the Biden plan to boost levies on corporations and top earners, as the key means to support critical infrastructure initiatives benefiting all Americans resonated with voters.

You may be familiar with something called the Gini Index or Coefficient, which measures a society's level of income or wealth distribution, with 1 representing maximal inequality and zero maximal equality. The US Census Bureau reported that income inequality reached its highest levels in over fifty years in 2018, with a Gini Index of .485 (up from .397 in 1967). That means that inequality in the US, even before the pandemic, was worse than in many emerging markets like Mexico (.454), Russia (.375), Argentina (.414), and Indonesia (.39), according to the World Bank. Another reality check: two of the only countries that are more unequal than the United States are Brazil and South Africa. If you still need convincing, you should know that inequality levels in specific states are even higher: New York, home to more billionaires than any other city in the world, records a Gini Index of over .51, almost on par with Brazil (.534).

And we know from the research of Keith Payne that inequality will ultimately adversely affect more than those at the shallow end of the wealth pool. In *The Broken Ladder*, Payne notes that inequality "makes us sick, unhappy, stressed out, and politically myopic. It undermines our performance and threatens our very democracies. The situation is not tenable."

Not surprisingly, inequality has a strong racial dimension. According to figures from the Federal Reserve Bank of St. Louis, the median wealth of an American Black family in 2019 was $23,000, equal to just 12 cents on the dollar of the median white family ($184,000). You might think that just getting a college degree could fix this, but the racial wealth gap persists even among more educated groups. A Black family with a member who's earned a bachelor's degree had roughly $51,000 in wealth in 2019, compared to $298,000 for white families and $77,000 for Hispanic families.

As was made abundantly clear in 2020, systemic inequality and institutional racism are still very much alive in America today. Black Americans make up around 13 percent of the US population, and yet over 20 percent of Americans in poverty are Black. Black Americans also account for a staggering 40 percent of the country's homeless population, while the proportion of Native Americans and Alaska Natives that are homeless is at least three times higher than their proportion of the general US population. Black men also make up around one-third of the country's prison population. The four-year graduation rate for Black students pursuing a bachelor's degree is 21 percent, compared to 32 percent for Hispanic students, 45 percent for white students, and 50 percent for Asian students. Research shows that Black Americans suspected of committing a crime are twice as likely to be killed by police officers than suspects of any other race.

When it comes to voting, people in a predominantly nonwhite area can expect to wait in line twice as long to vote as people in a majority-white area, which one researcher argues is because election administrators send more booths and polling workers to white areas. To see this in action, look no further than Georgia, where Black voters reported waiting for more than five hours to vote in the 2020 presidential election. But the extraordinary effort led by former gubernatorial candidate Stacey Abrams to register 800,000 new voters in the Peach State may well have paid off, inasmuch as Joe Biden was the first Democratic presidential candidate to carry Georgia since Bill Clinton in 1992. And the Herculean task ultimately led to two Senate wins for the Democrats, even though unacceptable race-based voting access discrepancies linger, and voting rights has become an ever more pressing partisan issue since the 2020 election.

We also now observe many manifestations of heightened "generational wars" between baby boomers and millennials, now joined by Generation Z. These wars aren't just about fashion choices, TikTok, and cultural attitudes. As I've noted, younger generations have found themselves in a much more precarious financial position than their parents. And there's data to prove it. In 2019, the St. Louis Fed found that median wealth for older families, headed by parents 65 to 75 years old, was $269,000, far more than the $24,000 held by the parents in millennial families (25–35 years old). The pandemic only made matters worse. In fact, the economic dislocation of COVID-19 has left millennials with the slowest economic growth of any generational cohort, and with less in savings and assets than previous generations had at their age.

Unfortunately, income inequality means much more than some of us having nicer houses and going on better vacations than others. It impacts everything from educational attainment and health outcomes, to job and financial security, to putting food on the table. In many US cities, including not only Baltimore and Cleveland but also the nation's capital (which ironically happens to be the country's richest city based on per capita income), fewer than 70 percent of students graduate from high school.

How is this possible given that these cities are home to not only prestigious universities but also a growing number of educated, professional young people? To give you some perspective, this means that secondary school graduation rates in these US cities are only slightly above national rates in Colombia and Mexico, and far behind those of other advanced economies like Ireland, South Korea, and Israel.

Aside from education, new research increasingly links poverty and inequality with negative health outcomes. Cardiologists believe that poverty is a factor in cardiovascular disease risk, as poorer communities tend to lack access to medical care and adequate health insurance (if they have any at all). The numerous maladies that can co-occur with such disease is also straining health services and local governments. Furthermore, poverty is linked with higher rates of obesity, since poorer individuals are often forced to rely on cheaper and less nutritious food over pricier and healthier alternatives. Obesity, as we know, is not only rising in the United States at alarming rates but is also tied to a number of serious conditions, including diabetes, hypertension, and heart disease.

Worse, we have seen how these conditions increase risks of dying from COVID-19, especially among people of color in the United States. For instance, Black, Hispanic, and Native Americans were hospitalized from COVID-19 at rates more than three times higher than whites, while COVID-19 death rates for these groups were also significantly higher. The US Centers for Disease Control and Prevention (CDC) blames discrimination, reduced access to healthcare and insurance, overrepresentation in exposed but essential "frontline" occupations and prisons, wealth gaps, and crowded housing as the primary drivers for this alarming discrepancy.

Thanks to the media and internet, this sense of income, wealth, and health inequality ricochets around the country and across the world with unprecedented intensity and speed, transmitted more graphically and universally than ever. This inequality is not sustainable, and it's no wonder many young people are today drawn to the socialist nostrums of the Bernie Sanderses of the world.

But if socialism is not the answer (and it's not), what is? Well, we should no longer expect a trickle-down, laissez-faire, Laffer Curve approach to economic growth to take care of the problem over time, as many politicians and economists started touting in the 1980s. Nor can we assume that vague calls for business and government to "work together" more closely will lead us to the land of milk and honey, and surely not as quickly or completely as needed. Business and government do need to work together more closely, but in highly specific and strategic ways that benefit all parties, especially the traditionally underserved.

Given the massive wealth creation of recent decades concentrated in the hands of the few, it's no surprise that we've been seeing a new twist on trickle-down economics: ever-growing celebrity-billionaire philanthropy that promises to "change the world" while generating tax breaks and positive publicity for the donors. As *The Guardian*'s Paul Vallely points out, the majority of big-ticket donations go to institutions that the wealthy themselves utilize, like elite universities. While there's no disputing the immense generosity of, say, Bill Gates and Melinda French Gates, philanthropic success or failure is hard to measure, and it's a field that largely operates outside public scrutiny. Even the Gates Foundation's laudable signature objective, eradicating malaria in our time, has proved elusive.

Former *New York Times* columnist Anand Giridharadas's recent book *Winners Take All: The Elite Charade of Changing the World* takes the view that we have been living in a new Gilded Age, where the rich, powerful, beautiful, and famous show off their ego-tripping charitable giving to "fight for equality and justice" and "to change the world," without meaningfully moving the needle—and while avoiding any fundamental change that might diminish or affect their clout, wealth, or interests. While I regard that view as unjustifiably harsh, I have to admit there are too few examples of major recent philanthropy-driven achievements or innovations in the world that can be traced back to the largely unseen billions spent or given away in the past decade or two.

Admittedly, most philanthropy, if rightly understood as a kind of high-risk, high-reward form of societal venture capital, fails. Look, for example, at more than a century of Rockefeller family philanthropy: we can laud their big wins (finding a cure for yellow fever; kick-starting the so-called Green Revolution to raise crop yields around the world; creating the University of Chicago on a barren Midway from the ground up) while giving them a pass on their mistakes, such as supporting eugenics during its heyday. But sadly most of their grants and programs over the decades have not had a transformative, sustainable impact commensurate with either their promise or their individual acts of immense generosity.

Philanthropists going back to the Medicis have used their giving and patronage to open doors and gain respectability, but the relatively recent case of convicted sex offender and late alleged mass-scale serial pedophile Jeffrey Epstein truly plumbed new lows. Epstein pocketed and skillfully deployed a fortune of shadowy origins that allowed him to rub shoulders with world leaders and high society while self-inventing a reputation for being a visionary "science philanthropist" by funding key programs at Harvard and MIT with his sprinkled millions. Harvard minted him a visiting fellow and gave him an office on campus but, even after his conviction, did not sever their close links to him. The fact that he lived in Manhattan's largest private residence only added to his one-time Gatsby-like mystique, showing that, more than ever, money can buy almost anything. No wonder that "average" people feel the deck is stacked against them, while those with wealth, even big-bucks grifters like Epstein, can get away with almost anything—an important, not-so-subtle subplot of the Trump era.

These are the kinds of disheartening stories that eat away at the country's mythical but immensely powerful and motivational Horatio Alger self-image, in which a decent American starting at the bottom can rise to the top through honest hard work and ingenuity. This is what always helped fuel that quintessential, cohesive, American can-do optimism that has been so central to its success. Americans once believed in the power of positive thinking, quoting the title of the perennial best-seller published by the Reverend Norman Vincent Peale in 1952. The book is still very much in print, but that sense of optimism has faded, and we need to get it back if we are to move the country forward.

Our optimistic pull toward ambitious goals, even without proof of the likelihood of success, has a home in the American philosophical school of pragmatism and the late-19th- and early-20th-century work of Charles Sanders Peirce, William James, and John Dewey. The thesis, perhaps best represented in James's work, advances the notion that choosing to believe in one's ability to achieve an ambitious goal not only provides a more purposeful and fulfilling life (versus the alternative of waiting for proof of the likelihood of success before pursuing one's ambition), but also makes achieving that goal more likely.

Contrast this notion that success is within one's reach with the increasingly sour taste of a winner-take-all economy that has helped set the stage for a series of colliding trends. Some of these trends are mutually reinforcing, as I've mentioned, helping to unleash our recent round of deglobalization, populism on the right and left, public discontent, and a general feeling that the "American Dream" (and other countries' equivalents) is dead.

This diminishing and uneven sense of American optimism about the future was readily apparent in a series of focus groups I hosted around the country back in 2015. In a study (discussed later in this book) envisioning what America might look like on the 250th anniversary of its founding, we asked different generational cohorts (boomers, Xers, and millennials) to tell us what they understood the "American Dream" to mean. Boomers (52–70 years of age at that time) had it down cold: they had lived lives of opportunity and were now ready to retire (or had retired) with a degree of financial security that exceeded their parents'. They were living the dream. Xers (then 36–51 years old) knew what the American Dream was, thought they had it in reach until the Great Recession hit, and now were wondering if they could get back on track to reaching it. But millennials (then 19–35 years old) had a very different narrative. Most who understood the term thought that it was beyond their grasp; some had given up any hope of even meeting their parents' level of economic attainment. One millennial actually had never heard the phrase "the American Dream" and guessed it was probably the name of a famous racehorse.

This anecdotal insight helps to underscore how generational inequality is diminishing optimism and shaping youth attitudes and intentions about the future. What clearly emerged from all these discussions across the length and breadth of America is that the unifying vision of the US as the land of opportunity—which has helped drive the country's performance since its founding—is very much at risk.

And these discussions took place five years before the global coronavirus pandemic had put a final coffin nail (tragically, literally) in the lives, hopes, and dreams of so many, conjuring up feelings of extreme anxiety, dread, alienation, despair, and smoldering anger on an unprecedented global scale. The CDC estimated that almost 40 percent of Americans had showed symptoms of anxiety disorder by year end 2020, up from only 8.2 percent during the first half of 2019.

Renaissance man Moisés Naím—bestselling author; Carnegie Endowment distinguished fellow; former business school dean; minister of trade and industry of Venezuela during that country's better days; and TV screenplay writer, producer, and personality—takes the view that these shocks and crises have revealed our world's "pre-existing conditions" and shaken us to the core. As he explains it: "What is very interesting in all of these crises is that a lot of what we thought was permanent—institutions, individuals, ideas, business models, ways of working—turned out to be transient, and new things that we believe were just temporary became normal." At Kearney, we are calling this "the Great Shakeout."

But this is not where the story needs to end, nor should we let it. Of course, not a few people worry we have allowed our institutions and democracy to decay and atrophy to such a degree that we are already beyond the point of no return.

As Australian-born London School of Economics professor Kenneth Minogue mused on the fall of past civilizations: "Islamic thinkers had an image for it. Consider a civilization based upon a court in a thriving city—Baghdad, for example. Arts and the intellect flourish. But over several generations . . . they lose their sharpness . . . And then some tribe of fierce [marauders], smelling out weakness, come thundering in from the desert and storm the city. As barbarians, they do not understand the usages of civilization. They stable their horses in the libraries and use sculptures as doorstops, pictures for target practice . . . This is the way the world goes. Sometimes it happens in one lifetime, as with those barbarian soldiers who rose to become Roman emperors, sometimes in slow motion, as with the fall of the Roman Empire, in which many centuries were to elapse before the new civilization emerged from the disorders of the barbarian invasions. With us, the decor is quite different, but the realities may be closer than we suppose."

While it's true that many past civilizations collapsed through weakness followed by eventual conquest from outside, I don't believe that is what awaits us. The weaknesses and rifts in our society and government represent a rot within, rather than an external enemy nipping at our heels, even if our adversaries have been only too willing to exploit our divisions and problems. But if I believed we were already past the point of no return, I wouldn't be writing this book.

So, please call me an optimist. I concur with Nicholas Kristof, the Pulitzer Prize–winning *New York Times* journalist and onetime Rhodes Scholar, and many others of comparable piercing insight, that the inflection point America has reached provides the opportunity for fundamental positive change. As Kristof puts it, "Overlapping catastrophes have also created conditions that may finally let us extricate ourselves from the mire. The grim awareness of national failures—on the coronavirus, racism, healthcare, and jobs—may be a necessary prelude to fixing our country. The last time our economy was this troubled, Herbert Hoover's failures led to Franklin Delano Roosevelt's election with a mandate to revitalize the nation. The result was the New Deal, Social Security, rural electrification, government jobs programs, and a 35-year burst of inclusive growth that built the modern middle class and arguably made the

United States the richest and most powerful country in the history of the world . . . So perhaps today's national pain, fear, and loss can also be a source of hope: We may be so desperate, our failures so manifest, our grief so raw, that the United States can once more, as during the Great Depression, embrace long-needed changes that would have been impossible in cheerier times."

To be sure, the results of the 2020 election felt like a let-down to many, as it appeared that the expected overwhelming national repudiation of Trump populism didn't happen. Astute observers and commentators pointed out that the razor-thin margins in various congressional and local races extended the phenomenon of a divided body politic and showed that Americans were more polarized than ever, each side only becoming more convinced of its own righteousness. These pundits have a point, but they forget that Joe Biden's winning popular-vote margin was larger than those of Harry Truman, John F. Kennedy, Richard Nixon, Jimmy Carter, Ronald Reagan during his first term, Bill Clinton, George W. Bush, and Donald Trump in 2016. And Joe Biden amassed more votes than any candidate in American history. The American people have spoken, even if not with an undivided voice: they chose a leader committed to unifying and healing a nation.

What the pundits also forget is that our country is no stranger to political divisions, and in fact some of our most remarkable achievements came during times of crisis. When our country was founded as a new republic, divisions had to be overcome with compromise and a mutual commitment to unity—a commitment that ensured our country and its revered institutions would last for generations. After the Civil War claimed the lives of more than 600,000 Americans, President Lincoln intended to foster unity and help the war-torn nation recover, an ambition tragically cut short by his assassination. The New Deal, launched to resolve what was then the country's worst economic crisis, was impelled by an optimistic leader, Franklin D. Roosevelt, who recognized that people were clamoring for relief and recovery. More recently, despite 1960s-era divisions stemming from the Civil Rights movement, the Vietnam

War, and urban riots, followed by the trauma of Watergate in the 1970s, America has proven again and again that we can survive dangers that many predicted would be our downfall.

Fast-forward to today's crisis-laden environment. President Biden, in the aftermath of the chaotic and bitterly contested 2020 election, had these reassuring words for the country after being declared President-elect: "[We need] to put the harsh rhetoric of the campaign behind us. To lower the temperature. To see each other again. To listen to each other again. To hear each other again. To respect and care for one another again. To unite. To heal. To come together again as a nation. I know this won't be easy. I'm not naïve . . . I know how deep and hard the opposing views are in our country on so many things. But I also know this as well: To make progress we must stop treating our opponents as our enemy. We are not enemies. What brings us together as Americans is stronger than anything that can tear us apart."

These last few years seem to have delivered a final blow to bipartisanship, and all significant initiatives from either side have been held hostage to the fierce opposition of the rival party, reducing our politics to an endless tug-of-war with few winners. Voters who pulled the lever in 2016 for the author of *The Art of the Deal* might have thought they would finally have a leader who could make important compromises in the country's best interest. Instead, they got four more years of continued deadlock on critical national policy questions ranging from immigration reform to investments in infrastructure investments and climate change. Whatever happened to reaching political compromise with legislators working across the aisle to come up with pragmatic solutions to the country's thorniest problems? Will the results of the 2020 election, which still seemed to show a very divided country despite giving control of the executive and legislative branches in Washington to the Democrats, force the new Congress and Executive branch of government, and Americans more generally, to find a workable way to coexist and advance?

In the Introduction, I explained how we have one past, one present, but multiple possible futures—and that no particular future is preordained, but rather it will be a function of the choices we make together. In this chapter, I've described a hellish, dystopian vision of the future that many people too easily assume is where we're headed: a nightmare sci-fi surveillance state marked by stark inequalities, scant opportunities for most people, worsening climate and disease crises, sporadic or even interminable wars, and internal unrest kept in check by heavy-handed (and heavily armed) authorities—mitigated only by offerings of "entertainment" designed to distract the populace and fill time, not unlike the "bread and circuses" of the Roman Empire in its decline. If that's the future, it's almost hardly worth sticking around for, even if human life spans resume their historic upward trend after recent drops (see chapter two).

But our future can be so much better than that. We all know about forecasting, but what about "backcasting"? Backcasting is actually an analytical tool by which you envision your desired future and work backward from that point to identify the steps needed to achieve it. How would you describe the kind of country (and world) you'd like to be living in, say, five, ten, or fifteen years from now? I know what my answer is, though I'll admit many may need a lot of convincing to believe a better future for all is still possible. Take a moment to imagine what you would regard as a much sunnier future. This book is written very much in that spirit, and over the course of the chapters ahead, I'll show you what a better future looks like, and how we might realistically get there. If you'd like a hint, take a peek at my four alternative visions of the future in chapter six. I want a robust *All-American Comeback*, and I believe that we can get there. I also believe we need to avoid becoming a depressed and depressing *Dollar Store America*—and I'm sure I'm not alone in that.

For too long, we have tried the same temporary Band-Aids, if we did anything at all, and look where it's gotten us. Einstein is said to have defined insanity as "doing the same thing over and over again and expecting different results." It's time for a change—for entirely new action. Tinkering won't do it anymore, if it ever did. A better future is not only possible, but also probable, if we embrace the specific new remedies and actions you'll be reading about in later chapters.

Globalization and the technological revolution of recent decades benefited many but also left behind a very large and angry underclass that's on the verge of becoming permanent. We must act to close this untenable and widening income and wealth gap, which is not only indefensible, but also a threat to social peace, prosperity, and democracy itself.

CHAPTER TWO

WHAT'S HOLDING
US BACK?

"An imbalance between rich and poor is the oldest
and most fatal ailment of all republics."
—PLUTARCH

"The causes which destroyed the ancient republics
were numerous; but in Rome, one principal
cause was the vast inequality of fortunes."
—NOAH WEBSTER

U ntil recently, the words "disruption" and "disruptors" had a
very positive connotation, at least in the corporate world. Brilliant techno-optimist (and XPRIZE founder) Peter Diamandis
describes the next few years as "what happens as AI, robotics, virtual
reality, digital biology, and sensors crash into 3D printing, blockchain,
and global gigabit networks."

This sounds great if you are well positioned, with the right education, skills, and capital, to benefit personally from the next rounds of
innovation, "creative destruction," and wealth creation. But what if
you're among the countless millions without the requisite background
to benefit from yet more "disruptive" change, and in fact are likely to see
your own life more derailed than improved?

That's the crux of the matter: the globalization and technological revolutions of recent decades have left behind a very large and increasingly permanent underclass in the West, stoking anger and frustration and boiling over into a populist revolt from below. This atmosphere of civil unrest could threaten our ability to address the very legitimate concerns that helped spawn that alienation and anger.

The Occupy and Tea Party movements were earlier warning signs of discontent. Falling living standards and decline of the white working class in America helped bring Donald Trump to the White House. Meanwhile, Black Lives Matter and the ensuing civil unrest of 2020 show the rage of an even more broadly and historically underserved segment of American society, which every day stares down racism in addition to the pernicious comorbidities of centuries-old poverty. These issues animated much of the 2020 urban voter turnout that—especially in critical states like Pennsylvania—was key to putting Joe Biden across the Electoral College finish line.

Inequality in America has been apparent throughout our history. President Lyndon Johnson's message to Congress in 1965 reminds us of this long-standing struggle: "There is really no part of America where the promise of equality has been fully kept. In Buffalo as well as in Birmingham, in Philadelphia as well as in Selma, Americans are struggling for the fruits of freedom." Acknowledging that the problems we're facing today are inextricably linked with the past, and reflective of it, may sound demoralizing. But just as previous generations did not give up on addressing these questions critical to our integrity and success, neither should we.

The plight of what politicians euphemistically call "working families" is literally a life-and-death matter. In addition to facing stalled social mobility, they are the left-behind, unemployed, or working poor, some of whom battle opioid addiction (rightly called "the problem from hell"), alcoholism, suicidal despair, falling life expectancy, and limited access to quality healthcare and education. Compounding these woes, many have little or no savings but plenty of high-interest credit card and other consumer debt in which they feel trapped. This is what the American Dream–turned-nightmare looks like to many of whom Harvard's Dani Rodrik calls the "immobile majority," and it's no more sustainable than it is morally defensible.

Princeton professors Anne Case and Angus Deaton have studied these indicators of decline, and their 2020 book *Deaths of Despair and the Future of Capitalism* makes for sobering—indeed, depressing—reading. The statistic they cite that I find the most troubling flashing red light is that life expectancy has been falling in the United States of late (a phenomenon predating the COVID-19 death toll). We have not seen such a modern-age reversal of mortality rates in any other advanced country since the 1918 flu pandemic. We should hang our heads in shame that our fellow citizens are literally dying from a combination of factors—including a lack of adequate healthcare—at the same time that the elite "mobile minority" enjoys both an unprecedented quality of life and a steadily increasing net worth. Worse, the already large wealth gap actually widened during the dark days of the COVID-19 pandemic.

My colleague Anne-Marie Slaughter, CEO of the think tank New America, wrote, "The biggest surprise of the pandemic is the national and global decoupling of the economy of the rich from the economy of everyone else." Bulgarian political scientist Ivan Krastev has made the point that just as the well-off could afford to globe-trot in normal times, "in the time of COVID-19, they can afford to stay at home," unlike so many ordinary people who haven't had the luxury of being able to telecommute—and who worked in the service sector or essential frontline jobs that left them very exposed.

Not surprisingly, just as America's mortality rates have increased, birth rates have dropped alarmingly: 2019 births totaled 3.75 million, the lowest level in over 35 years, according to the CDC. Census data show that the 2010s were marred by particularly slow population growth. While changing attitudes toward family and birth delays are factors—in addition to a general sense of angst and uncertainty about the future—precarious finances are also a culprit, as fewer feel that they can afford to support a family. As the long-term effects of the coronavirus take their toll on the global economy, birth rates may well continue falling, creating extended problems for aging people worldwide.

In the last chapter, I cited some depressing statistics about how measures of inequality in America increasingly resemble what you would expect to see in what we used to call Third World countries, not rich and advanced ones. This slide has only accelerated. The latest Social Progress Index, based on 50 metrics of well-being and quality of life and grounded on the work of Nobel Prize–winning economists, shows that the United States, Brazil, and Hungary are the only nations in which people are worse off than when the index began tracking these factors in 2011.

Michael Porter, the star Harvard Business School professor who is the index's advisory panel head, said, "The data paint an alarming picture of the state of our nation, and we hope it will be a call to action . . . It's like we're a developing country . . . We are no longer the country we like to think we are." America, notwithstanding all its advantages, today ranks 28th, having slipped from 19th when the Social Progress Index debuted.

Nicholas Kristof of the *New York Times* says, "The Social Progress Index finds that Americans have health statistics similar to those of people in Chile, Jordan and Albania, while kids in the United States get an education roughly on par with what children get in Uzbekistan and Mongolia." He also states: "The United States ranks No. 1 in the world in quality of universities, but No. 91 in access to quality basic education. The US leads the world in medical technology, yet we are No. 97 in access to quality health care."

But even America's preeminent position in higher education is at risk, given the decline in university enrollment among the world's best and brightest, who worry about an increasingly tattered welcome mat for students from abroad. I recall not too long ago visiting with an America-loving Middle Eastern friend who hosted a dinner for me with a half dozen of his equally successful compatriots. Each of them had studied in the US and had leveraged that education into quite successful careers, for which they professed profound gratitude to America and Americans.

However, every one of them was advising their children not to study in the US as they had, arguing sadly that the xenophobia emerging in the past five years posed too troubling an environment to which they could entrust their children. America's policies and cultural practices of openness and welcome, on which the country was founded and which prompted its growth and greatness, are at risk.

America's powerhouse universities and graduate schools are matchless in their prestige, financial resources, and drawing power, and up to now have been the most sought after by the brightest and most ambitious students the world over. Likewise, America's top teaching hospitals, starting with the Mayo Clinic and Johns Hopkins, are simply without equals elsewhere, and elites from around the world come to them for their medical care. For example, the ruling family of Abu Dhabi entrusts its health to the world-class professionals and facilities of the Johns Hopkins Medical Institutions in Baltimore, and has generously given enormous gifts, including funds for the hospital's state-of-the-art Sheikh Zayed Tower. Yet all this cutting-edge research and exceptional care takes place within a particularly depressed area of Baltimore, a city where many struggle with addiction, HIV, and even tuberculosis, and where very few have access to these "local" paragons of medicine.

Sadly, most Americans throughout the country never experience healthcare at anything remotely close to that quality, if they even have access to decent basic healthcare at all. More than ever, we seem to be two Americas: one offering the best of the best of everything to those with the means to afford it; and, for the rest, a big plunge in the quality and availability of even essential services.

These kinds of growing and gaping disparities are simply untenable, but before you think I'm going socialist on you, I'm anxious to point out that the world's first national health insurance, accident, disability, and pension plans were set up by the arch-conservative German chancellor Otto von Bismarck in the 1880s, as a way of trying to make capitalism work for all citizens by giving them a sense of security about their lives, families, and futures. The Iron Chancellor, author of the much-quoted line that lawmaking, like sausage making, is not an appetizing sight, was no Pollyannaish social innovator, but rather a sober realist. Bismarck, who apparently even had a sense of humor, quipped: "Never believe anything until it has been officially denied."

Have we so devolved over the last century and a half that we can't also understand and do what needs to be done in our own best collective interest? Surely in the 2020s we can find new and even better ways to give people a sense of security, stability, hope, and predictability for their lives.

The phenomenon I'm describing is certainly not limited to the United States. The same underlying problems and frustrations brought about Brexit, swept populists into office the world over from Brasília to Budapest, and sent people with grievances into the streets en masse. France's mostly working-class *gilets jaunes* in their signature yellow vests; Hong Kong youths' demands for civil liberties; protests in countries from Chile to Lebanon over government corruption, high food prices, and lack of opportunity; Black Lives Matter–spawned protests seeking an end to racial discrimination in cities around the globe; even those forever-Trumpers on the other side of the barricades—people are, in the parlance of an old movie, "mad as hell and they're not gonna take this anymore."

The "shrinking center" and polarization to harder right and left— common trends across many countries—haven't helped, either. The culture wars between progressives and social conservatives have shown us that many people no longer see much common ground with their fellow citizens. Indeed, there are issues on which people with radically different views will never find unity. However, healthy democracies can and do find ways to reconcile such fundamental differences of opinion and conscience. For instance, some scholars suggest that teaching young students how to engage in civil, constructive debate could help mitigate some of these problems in the coming years. But for the moment, our body politic has been cracking under the strain of these and other rifts. The lines that Irish poet W. B. Yeats penned in 1919 in the wake of the horrors of the First World War seem more relevant than ever: "Things fall apart; the centre cannot hold . . . The best lack all conviction, while the worst / Are full of passionate intensity." Destroying truth and trust can be done very quickly, but restoring it is a slow and daunting task.

And our society longs not only for decency, but also for a return to civility—beginning with civilized debate. Today we have shouting matches, ad hominem attacks, and an enforced ideological conformity on both extremes of the political spectrum—even the specter of Orwellian "thoughtcrime." So it's perhaps not surprising that in President Biden's first speech to the nation as president, he firmly said, "We must end this uncivil war." Of course, it is worth noting that today's lack of decorum, as bad as it is and as much as it needs to improve, pales in comparison to violence that prevailed in the US Congress just prior to the Civil War. In her fascinating historical account of those tumultuous antebellum days between 1830 and 1860, Joanne B. Freeman recounts "more than 70 violent incidents between congressmen in the House and Senate chambers and on nearby streets and dueling grounds." Of course, that period of uncivil discourse did slide us into the bloodiest war in American history, a fate we must never repeat. Even so, 2021 did open with a return of violent mob scenes to the hallowed halls of Congress (and to state capitols) that shocked the world.

Amid this atmosphere of division, in July 2020, some of the world's leading authors, academics, journalists, and thought leaders across a broad range of views, if perhaps weighted to the left of center, signed a public "Letter on Justice and Open Debate" in collaboration with *Harper's* magazine, defending the right to free speech against excessive political correctness whatever its origins or intentions, and hoping to help jump-start a more civil discourse. Prominent signatories included Anne Applebaum, Margaret Atwood, Noam Chomsky, Francis Fukuyama, Malcolm Gladwell, Michael Ignatieff, Garry Kasparov, Steven Pinker, J. K. Rowling, Sir Salman Rushdie, Gloria Steinem, and Fareed Zakaria. The letter sparked not only support, but also some controversy and pushback, unleashing a comprehensive debate over modern "cancel culture" and whether free speech is jeopardized in today's world. That a letter about free speech sparked a debate over whether or not it is in jeopardy shows the central role that open and honest debate plays in our society. This further underscores the hunger for genuinely civilized and informed debate, which is good for society and needed now more than ever.

And, frankly, it wasn't so long ago that we had such civilized and informed policy debates across party lines. I recall my days in the US Senate as then-Senator Joe Biden's legislative director when partisanship almost always took a back seat to advancing national interests. In my judgment, that civil discourse and cross-aisle collaboration began to fray when congressional deliberations began being televised. Though a laudable objective in the interest of transparency, I began to observe members of Congress speaking to the camera more than to their colleagues, intent on making a splash to command airtime on the nightly network news. And, of course, this trend away from non-newsworthy compromise has been compounded exponentially with the advent of social media. When the final chapter is written about the 2016 and 2020 elections, social media's impact no doubt will be judged quite substantial. Even though major platforms like Twitter and Facebook somewhat belatedly attempted to monitor and police their sites against false and misleading claims, much misinformation still fed false narratives about candidate positions, likely influencing voter behavior and sowing further division.

During a notable 2020 campaign stop at Gettysburg, Joe Biden had these words for the country:

> There is no more fitting place than here today in Gettysburg to talk about the cost of division—about how much it has cost America in the past, about how much it is costing us now, and about why I believe in this moment we must come together as a nation . . . Here, on this sacred ground, Abraham Lincoln reimagined America itself . . . Today, once again, we are a house divided. But that, my friends, can no longer be. We are facing too many crises. We have too much work to do. We have too bright a future to leave it shipwrecked on the shoals of anger and hate and division . . . As I look across America today, I'm concerned. The country is in a dangerous

place. Our trust in each other is ebbing. Hope is elusive. Too many Americans see our public life not as an arena for the mediation of our differences. Rather, they see it as an occasion for total, unrelenting partisan warfare . . . We need to revive a spirit of bipartisanship in this country, a spirit of being able to work with one another . . . In his Second Inaugural, Lincoln said, "With malice toward none, with charity for all, with firmness in the right as God gives us to see the right, let us strive on to finish the work we are in, to bind up the nation's wounds." Now we have our work to reunite America, to bind up the nation's wounds, to move past shadow and suspicion.

As for that open letter in *Harper's*, were George Orwell alive today, I strongly suspect he would have been one of the signatories in favor of free speech and civil discourse. As for the "merits" of policing and constricting speech on campus and elsewhere, Orwell would probably repeat what he said about some similarly ill-advised things and exaggerated trends in his own day: "You have to be an intellectual to believe something like that. No ordinary man could be such a fool."

While some protestors have railed against the "top 1 percent," British-born Brookings Institution scholar Richard Reeves isn't worried so much about the super-rich in that tier, but rather about the top 20 percent of the US population who believe they got there by merit, yet in fact increasingly form a hereditary upper-middle class that intermarries and "hoards" the American Dream through its many cumulative advantages.

As late as 2016, we saw the appearance of a bestselling book in the US called *The Upside of Inequality*, by Bain Capital founding partner and close Mitt Romney associate Edward Conard. To Conard, high inequality is actually a sign of American economic health and innovation, as very high financial payoffs for successful risk-taking create strong incentives for growth. No sensible person I know wants to take away incentives from innovators, but I really wonder whether such a thesis could carry any weight now, given what America and the world have been through in the last few years. Conard, and many with similar views since the 1980s, celebrates the success of self-made billionaires but offers little in the way of ideas to help those struggling in the bottom half of society. Our collective failure to address those problems has now come home to roost with a vengeance. I'd go so far as to say that, in its most unbridled form, the laissez-faire "religion" has proved itself obsolete.

Joel Kotkin, a noted California academic and urbanist, strikes an even more pessimistic chord than many other analysts in his recent book, *The Coming of Neo-Feudalism: A Warning to the Global Middle Class.* According to Kotkin, our previous decades of expansion of wealth and opportunity have ended, and we are almost inevitably returning toward a new "feudal" era marked by great concentration of wealth and property and reduced upward mobility. In his view,

> if the last seventy years saw a massive expansion of the middle class, not only in America but in much of the developed world, today that class is declining and a new, more hierarchical society is emerging. The new class structure resembles that of Medieval times. At the apex of the new order are two classes—a reborn clerical elite, the clerisy, which dominates the upper part of the professional ranks, universities, media and culture, and a new aristocracy led by tech oligarchs with unprecedented wealth and growing control of information.

Below these two classes lies what was once called the Third Estate in ancien régime Europe. This includes what Kotkin calls the new "Yeomanry," a group made up largely of small-business people, minor property owners, skilled workers, and lower-level private-sector professionals—in effect, the declining middle class. Below them are growing numbers of new "Serfs," a vast, expanding, property-less population lacking even modest savings, education, or anything other than low-paying service industry jobs—if they're employed at all. It's a dark vision, perhaps made all the darker in the wake of the pandemic's economic dislocation, and there is more than a little truth in Kotkin's analysis. He's not so pessimistic, however, to think that it's too late to prevent this emerging neo-feudalism from becoming a permanent reality.

Some point to unapologetic shareholder capitalism as one reason behind such growing inequality. When companies only care about profits and shareholders over the well-being of workers, the community, and the environment, vast inequality naturally follows. More and more businesses have expressed interest in "stakeholder capitalism" to replace this outdated shareholder model. While this shift is admirable, early indicators show that too few companies have actually changed practices to align with these lofty goals.

In the year 2000, star journalist and commentator David Brooks both celebrated and poked fun at the new elite that was rapidly displacing the old WASP Eastern establishment and the 1980s Yuppie generation in his runaway bestseller *Bobos in Paradise*. While Brooks didn't coin the term "Bobos" for "Bourgeois Bohemians" (it was already in use in France), he applied it to the emergent, highly affluent class of Americans who combined smarts, ambition, and worldly success with a carefully cultivated self-image of free-spirit rebels channeling the coolest collective memories of 1960s counterculture. Other observers noticed the same phenomenon, including urban studies scholar and author Richard Florida, who dubbed them the new "Creative Class."

Brooks's and others' wry descriptions of this new, meritocratic, Ivy-degreed elite—wearing yoga pants, zipping around in expensive electric cars, shopping at Whole Foods, and sipping small-batch, artisanal, hand-roasted coffees—captured the mood and zeitgeist at the turn of the millennium and beyond. If members of this new class thought at all about lesser mortals, it was to recoil in horror at their relatively dingy and pathetic lives. Brooks found the *New York Times* Sunday-edition weddings section the perfect summation of their tastes and values: "When you look at the *Times* wedding page, you can almost feel the force of the mingling SAT scores . . . an amazing number of [newlywed couples] seem to have met while recovering from marathons . . . or on archeological digs in Eritrea."

Twenty years later, Brooks finds the gulf between university-bred coastal elites and the left-behind working-class heartland "deplorables" anything but funny and feels that unless a new sense of national solidarity and common purpose can be found, bitter culture wars will continue tearing the United States to pieces. Richard Florida, too, has more recently written in 2017 about the downside of the success of the Creative Class, who, in making "superstar cities" playgrounds for the rich and affluent like themselves, have unintentionally helped create a new urban crisis with increasing unaffordability, inequality, and segregation separating the flourishing elite from the rest. Both Brooks and Florida feel that this unsustainable divide has reached a crisis point. David Brooks wrote in July 2020:

> The New Dealers succeeded in a moment like this. Their experience offers some powerful lessons . . . Economic and health calamities are experienced by most people as if they were natural disasters and complete societal breakdowns. People feel intense waves of fear about the future. They want a leader, like FDR, who demonstrates optimistic fearlessness . . . They want one who, once in office, produces an intense burst of activity that is both new but also offers people security and safety . . . New Dealers were willing to try anything that met the specific emergencies of the moment. There was a strong anti-ideological bias in the administration and a wanton willingness to experiment. For example, Roosevelt's first instinct was to cut government spending in order to reduce the deficit, until he flipped, realizing that it wouldn't work in a depression. "I really do not know what the basic principle of the New Deal is," one of his top advisors admitted. That pragmatism reassured the American people, who didn't want a revolution; they wanted a recovery.

Let me put it bluntly: unless we are ready to open our eyes and grapple with the legitimate grievances and pervasive problems of our "left-behind" fellow citizens in that very American spirit of pragmatic, can-do optimism, we may have to live with explosive politics and civil unrest on an ongoing, indeed permanent, basis, with catastrophic and corrosive long-term consequences. This is the very definition of a zero-sum game that will leave everyone worse off.

Austrian-born Stanford professor Walter Scheidel believes "inequality never dies peacefully," but I'll only agree with him up to a point. In Scheidel's view, the "four horsemen" of leveling that have historically decreased inequality by substantial levels are all violent events: wars, revolutions, plagues, and state or societal collapses—catastrophes that upend old orders, often in bloody or deadly ways. Such ways of decreasing inequality tend to leave everyone worse off and sow the seeds for the next tumult. As I've previously said, unless we tackle inequality in America, our politics and society will continue to be very combustible and fractious. However, my ongoing hope is that our coronavirus "plague" experience—converging with the other three existential threats that create urgent imperatives to generate inclusive economic growth, reverse climate change, and establish racial justice—will be a sufficient catalyst (and gut punch) for real change and improvement. Real change and progress will stave off more volatile, drastic, and ultimately unproductive anger-fueled reactions, much as the Great Depression brought us the New Deal and not the socialist revolution that was brewing.

Just to be clear: wealth creation isn't the issue, as we're still creating wealth at a fast clip—it's just unevenly distributed. Irish-born Silicon Valley guru and Santa Fe Institute fellow W. Brian Arthur predicts, "We will move from an economy where the main challenge is to produce more and more efficiently to one where distribution of the wealth produced becomes the biggest issue."

Brian, who broke new ground in our understanding of how network effects of scale create truly outsized increasing returns for the likes of the FAANGs (Facebook, Apple, Amazon, Netflix, and Google), thinks AI is "the biggest thing since the printing press in the 1450s." That's quite a statement from someone who has studied the history of technology from the steam engine and early railway boom to the Internet. Brian's view is that what he calls the oncoming AI-driven "autonomous economy" of "algorithms in conversation with other algorithms, making decisions" will, quantitatively, create more wealth for the few than it creates good, stable jobs for the many. Though he believes societies will eventually adjust over decades, that's a problem—and frankly we can't wait that long to replenish middle-class hopes and opportunities.

The public may well have already caught on. In a recent version of the Edelman Trust Barometer, a key gauge of public opinion I'll be telling you more about later in the book, the average American worries that technology is a bigger threat to their employment and livelihood than immigration. (However, listening to the political "dialogue" around immigration issues, one would never know that public opinion has so shifted!)

Big tech companies, moreover, are coming under increasing fire (and litigation) as they amass wealth and market power, often without exercise of sufficient restraint on the misuse and abuse of their platforms by agents provocateurs, both foreign and domestic, with sinister intentions. In 2020, the House of Representatives investigated whether Apple, Amazon, Google, and Facebook hold monopoly power in the market. This was the Democrats' finding: "To put it simply, companies that were once scrappy, underdog startups that challenged the status quo have become the kinds of monopolies we last saw in the era of oil barons and railroad tycoons." The report advises increasing congressional oversight over these companies, arguing that these firms now have far too much power. In late 2020, the US Federal Trade Commission and dozens of states went as far as suing Facebook for allegedly illegal anticompetitive behavior, calling for the company to be broken up, including through the divestment of Instagram and WhatsApp. In addition, the US Justice Department sued Google for violating antitrust laws in October 2020, and numerous states followed suit.

Going back to the House Democrats' report, its authors even quoted the late Supreme Court justice Louis Brandeis: "We must make our choice. We may have democracy, or we may have wealth concentrated in the hands of a few, but we cannot have both." Justice Brandeis, who made fighting perilous inequality and monopolies the centerpiece of his legal career, could not have known that his words would be so relevant today.

So these are not new issues. In fact, Aristotle wrote over two millennia ago to emphasize the importance of creating and maintaining a large middle class as the basis for a stable and healthy society: "It is clear then that the best partnership in a state is the one which operates through the middle people, and also that those states in which the middle element is large, and stronger if possible than the other two together, or at any rate stronger than either of them alone, have every chance of having a well-run constitution."

We have a long tradition of recognizing the ill that rampant inequality can cause in the United States. In 1910, while speaking in Kansas, President Teddy Roosevelt advocated for corporations to have less power, and that the rules of the game needed to be fair so everyone can compete. As he so eloquently put it: "In every wise struggle for human betterment one of the main objects, and often the only object, has been to achieve in large measure equality of opportunity. In the struggle for this great end, nations rise from barbarism to civilization, and through it people press forward from one stage of enlightenment to the next. One of the chief factors in progress is the destruction of special privilege." Roosevelt then added that equal opportunity benefits *everyone,* even those who may have to give something up, like tax breaks.

According to Roosevelt, societies without special privileges are not just fairer, but also more beneficial, as everyone is able to perform to his or her best ability. Someone from West Baltimore or the South Bronx or LA's Skid Row might be able to find the cure for the next pandemic or do some other amazing thing if given a solid education and the same chance at success as everyone else. At the moment, so much human capital and potential goes to waste. This means that all of us, even those who have largely benefited from the existing economic patterns of the past 30 years, stand to gain if everyone gets a fair shot.

I for one believe a better future for all is possible, including renewed middle-class dreams, and in later chapters I'll try to show how we can get there. In one of my alternative visions of the future, which I address in chapter six, the United States makes an *All-American Comeback* by continuing to support innovation and growth while recognizing that its benefits must be distributed fairly. In the next section, though, I'll reflect on our history to show how we got here and how we can move beyond where we are. Speaking of history, I leave you with a quote often attributed to one of America's greatest admirers and observers, Winston Churchill, as I believe he put it best: "You can always count on Americans to do the right thing—after they've tried everything else."

PART 2

WHY A BETTER FUTURE IS POSSIBLE

Now that I've given you an overview of where things are today—and why we're not doomed to live in some disaster movie—let's turn back the clock and see how previous generations overcame seemingly intractable problems and moved beyond their own disaster scenarios. I know that to many it seems like the challenges we're facing are insurmountable, but the world has faced many crises and disasters before. In fact, on many occasions when history has presented past leaders with a wealth of challenges, humanity has not only overcome them, but actually built stronger societies in the process. Especially for younger readers, it's important to remember that some of the world's most shining moments came after times of immense crisis. So enough with the nihilism—let's look back on our past not only to learn about how we got here, but also to see more clearly how we can get out of the seeming rut we've been in.

CHAPTER THREE

On September 11, 2001, the United States suffered the deadliest terrorist attacks in human history. Thousands of lives were lost, and the world was changed forever. But after this tragedy, we rebuilt—just as human beings have always done.

HUMANITY IS RESILIENT, AND SO IS THE UNITED STATES— JUST STUDY HISTORY

"Life must be lived forward, but it can only be understood backwards."
—**KIERKEGAARD**

"The only thing new in the world is the history you don't know."
—**HARRY TRUMAN**

". . . I have never been more confident or more optimistic about America."
—**PRESIDENT JOSEPH R. BIDEN** *IN ADDRESS TO JOINT SESSION OF CONGRESS; APRIL 2021*

It's crucial that we put our current crises and disasters into some historical context. My parents lived through the Great Depression and the Second World War, and I came of age during the outsized shocks and malaise of Vietnam, assassinations, race riots, Watergate, the '70s oil crisis, and stagflation. In fact, it's been so long since we simultaneously experienced high inflation with economic stagnation and record unemployment—things we think normally don't go together—that few remember how awful stagflation was, or can be.

But humanity bounces back, as it did from the horrors of the 20th century, including two world wars, the Holocaust, the Cold War, the once ever-present threat of nuclear Armageddon, and 9/11. So, it's good to step back and put today's fundamental challenges into perspective.

We *can* overcome our present problems, but it will take leaders demonstrating real leadership; fresh ideas; and new, coordinated, and courageous action on many levels. We also need a motivated and engaged "followership" prepared to demand and get better leadership that provides the right policy prescriptions to address unmet needs. These are conditions not beyond our reach, despite what has appeared to be an irreconcilable series of societal divisions, which some have seized on and inflamed to advance their own interests.

We need to reverse that perverse manipulation of real human needs to ensure that the collective trauma of the pandemic, its economic and societal shockwaves, and its lingering effects become the cathartic impetus to address basic human needs. Organizations and societies on the verge of *breakdowns* are usually those most capable of *breakthroughs*. Breakthroughs are what happen when people and organizations are shaken out of their complacency and begin to think creatively and see challenges as opportunities. The key is how you manage to turn breakdowns into breakthroughs. Throughout my 50-year career, 1 have had the opportunity to see and work with organizations confronting profound, even existential, threats. Some rise to the challenge and reinvent themselves according to change imperatives lurking just over the horizon, while other, seemingly less-challenged competitors lull themselves into extinction with a false sense of security that comes from not understanding or accepting the need to transform.

For instance, forward-looking, Denmark-based DONG Energy, once an oil and gas company, rightly noted that wind power—and renewables more generally—was set to become the next big thing in energy. The company undertook a complete transformation, selling its oil and gas business and focusing instead on wind and solar power. You might know this company by its new name, Ørsted, today the world's largest offshore wind developer.

On the flip side, remember the once-omnipresent video-rental chain Blockbuster? Unfortunately for its employees and shareowners, the company failed to adapt to new competition from Netflix and the challenge of video streaming and declared bankruptcy in 2010 before attempting several ill-fated reorganizations. Of this former colossus of nearly ten thousand stores around the world, today there remains only one lonely Blockbuster store, in Bend, Oregon, which has a franchise right to use the brand name. It survives thanks to hyper-local, very personal service combined with a dose of 1990s nostalgia; you can even rent the place for a movie night sleepover on Airbnb.

Human beings regroup and rebuild; that's what we've always done and can do again. Societies and institutions of all kinds have already resolved immense challenges by steering breakdowns to breakthroughs. Those that don't miss historic opportunities to advance at best; at worst, they collapse.

UCLA scientist and MacArthur Foundation Genius Award fellow Jared Diamond has studied societies under great strain from ancient times to the present day, and his book *Collapse: How Societies Choose to Fail or Succeed* has been a global bestseller. As the title suggests, societal failure and regeneration are *choices,* not preordained outcomes. Diamond notes that Easter Island's monoliths, Central America's Mayan city ruins, and Cambodia's Angkor Wat complex are eerie reminders that bad decisions have provoked the fall of once-thriving civilizations. However, good decisions in the face of immense challenges can reboot societies on the knife-edge of resurgence or decline.

Take the example of China, once centuries ahead of Europe and the world's largest economy (as it hopes and expects to be again). During the time of Europe's Dark Ages, China's Song Dynasty ushered in a period of open trade with the wider world, technological invention, and even a kind of very early industrial revolution with such innovations as the compass, paper money, and water-powered textile machines. Later dynasties, however, turned inward, and China not only lost its lead, but also fell far behind. The Ming Dynasty may be famous for its pottery, but it banned overseas trade and restricted internal movement. The final dynasty, called Qing or Manchu, which eventually collapsed in 1912, turned China into a nation of ever greater stagnation and isolation. In 1661, it even forced a large southern coastal population to move some 30 kilometers inland as part of its emphatic inward turn away from the outside world.

Few know that at its apogee, China had not only the world's largest economy, but also the globe's largest city—Beijing, with over a million people—when European capitals were still comparatively small. It even had the world's largest ocean-going navy, with all these imperial institutions run by a meritocratic class of "mandarins" (civil servants) who achieved their positions by competitive exam.

China's historical example teaches at least two lessons. First, isolationism and a closed-border mentality—the very opposite of openness to the world and its ideas, peoples, advances, goods, and services—is a sure recipe for decline, if not disaster. And second, the climb back to prosperity and relevance is steep and long, even if there is the national will to build back. It's sometimes claimed that the Chinese invented gunpowder but used it mostly for fireworks. That's not entirely accurate, as this Chinese invention was also used for early weapons in Asia. But with China's turn inward, Europeans made much more use of gunpowder, conquering and colonizing much of the world with the aid of cannons and muskets, and eventually still more advanced weapons. This is not to suggest that Europeans' wars and conquests are to be lauded, but rather to show that shutting out the world as China did had profoundly negative consequences for the Middle Kingdom.

Clearly not all struggling countries or civilizations turn the corner and manage to regenerate or even survive. We would do well to remind ourselves that it takes many generations, even centuries or millennia, to build up societies and institutions, but that they can be destroyed or irreparably damaged very quickly. In the last century, people asked this about Germany: How could the cultured nation of Goethe and Beethoven become Hitler's brutal Third Reich so swiftly, turning a land of "poets and thinkers" (*Dichter und Denker*) into one of "judges and hangmen" (*Richter und Henker*) in such a short time?

We must never allow ourselves to become complacent and think our own founding ideals and hallowed institutions are rock solid and unbreakable. Poet T. S. Eliot, a literary genius with a deep knowledge of history and culture, had his own lyrical way of describing what it would be like to try to rebuild once your country or civilization had come apart and hit rock bottom: "Then you must start painfully again, and you cannot put on a new culture ready made. You must wait for the grass to grow to feed the sheep to give you the wool of which your new coat will be made." Like Diamond, Eliot took the view that rebuilding from societal collapse, if it happens at all, usually takes a long time—generations.

And clearly it will take some time and distance from the damage inflicted on American democratic institutions by Trumpism, and those forces that led to its rise, to be able to tell when those institutions—so critical to our social stability and progress—might fully regenerate. One hopes that Joe Biden's conviction will prove correct: that four years of Donald Trump as president will be seen as an aberration from which we can recover. But restoring those institutions will require, as Tom Friedman of the *New York Times* has noted, "truth and trust," both of which have been in short supply of late, yet are at the very heart of the Biden promise. But, as I've noted, restoring truth and trust will take time.

But let's rewind again to the depths of the Great Depression to give ourselves some perspective on how this kind of more positive outcome can come about by addressing problems in the nick of time. In the United States in the early 1930s, industrial production contracted by 46 percent, foreign trade fell by 70 percent, and unemployment increased by over 600 percent—peaking in 1933 at 25 percent officially, but with the true rate of un- and underemployment even higher. Soup kitchens for the middle class and the phrase "Buddy, can you spare a dime?" were all too common. The US was on the verge of collapse, the American Dream was in tatters, and a socialist class consciousness was taking root.

The last time the United States had faced such colossal difficulties was in the previous century, during and after the American Civil War. The period known as the Reconstruction Era (1865–1877) was a time to repair and regenerate a country that was materially devastated, still bitter and divided, and struggling against continuing opposition to giving freed slaves their full and proper constitutional rights as US citizens. But the cliff-edge catastrophe facing the US in the early 1930s was without precedent, and also part of the first truly global and simultaneous economic and financial crisis.

Enter FDR. His leadership and the New Deal, though vilified by many of the elite at the time, lifted spirits immediately and soon brought America back from the edge of the abyss. Franklin Roosevelt transformed a breakdown into a breakthrough. As *The Economist* wrote, "You can change the course of history through force of will." The new president was up against enormous odds. As historian Anthony Badger wrote of that period, "many Americans doubted the capacity of a democratic government to act decisively enough to save the country."

The fresh memory of the Russian Revolution of 1917, the spread of uprisings throughout Europe, fears of communism rooting in the US, and, not least, the need to protect an increasingly desperate citizenry, moved our leaders to launch the New Deal. These policies, aimed at providing basic financial security and hope for so many who had hit rock bottom, were what preempted social upheaval—much like similar programs in Bismarck's Germany, except on a much bigger, bolder scale. The litany of FDR's innovations is long: the Social Security Act, the Fair Labor Standards Act, the Federal Deposit Insurance Corporation, the Securities and Exchange Commission, the US Housing Authority, the Farm Security Administration, the Tennessee Valley Authority . . . all these made the new social compact with the average working American clear and compelling.

But before Roosevelt could affect fundamental policy change, he needed to transmit a sense of optimism at a time when not only the stability of the American Republic was at risk, but also the very fate of Western civilization. California Republican senator Hiram Johnson summed up the FDR effect by noting that "the admirable trait in Roosevelt is that he has the guts to try. He does it all with the rarest good nature . . . We have exchanged a frown in the White House for a smile. Where there was hesitation and vacillation, weighing always the personal political consequences, feebleness, timidity and duplicity, there are now courage and boldness for real action." Sound familiar?

David Brooks, whom I quoted earlier, says that the New Deal was much more comprehensive than simply taxes and expenditure, which is what made it so successful. Brooks notes that government agencies like the Reconstruction Finance Corporation and Federal Housing Administration (FHA) incentivized banks to lend capital while backing mortgages. The result was higher levels of lending: in just a few months, the amount of private lending stimulated by the FHA was actually larger than the funds the otherwise notable Public Works Administration would spend over a decade. As Brooks puts it, "The New Deal brought balance . . . [It] didn't produce an instant economic turnaround. But it did show that democratic capitalism could still function."

According to Brooks, the New Deal was also successful because it was well run. FDR selected top-notch lawyers, economists, professors, and social workers. FDR himself also faced tremendous pressure from the more radical populists within his party, but his talent, and that of his team, stopped them from shaping policy. Like previous presidents including Abraham Lincoln and Theodore Roosevelt, FDR passed the most progressive legislation in the nation's history to that point as a centrist. As Brooks says, "FDR was able to pass so much legislation precisely because he was so shifting and pragmatic and did not turn everything into a polarized war . . . in a time of crisis, in an ideological age, he showed it's possible to get a lot done if you turn down the ideological temperature, if you evade the culture war, if you are willing to be positive and openly experimental." Time will tell if patriotic collaboration can overcome partisan posturing.

Joe Biden probably best signaled his own authentic FDR-like pragmatic demeanor with some of his first words addressed to the American public after being declared president-elect: "The refusal of Democrats and Republicans to cooperate with one another is not due to some mysterious force beyond our control. It's a decision. It's a choice we make. And if we can decide not to cooperate, then we can decide to cooperate. And I believe that this is part of the mandate from the American people. They want us to cooperate. That's the choice I'll make. And I call on the Congress—Democrats and Republicans alike—to make that choice with me."

FDR's approach was actually so experimental and unorthodox that he quietly engineered an American default so subtle that we hardly remember it now, according to Sebastián Edwards, who's written an excellent book (called, unsurprisingly, *American Default: The Untold Story of FDR, the Supreme Court, and the Battle over Gold*) about this long-forgotten episode. Sebastián, a "Chicago Boy" economist and Henry Ford II Professor at the UCLA Anderson School of Management, explains what happened:

> The American economy is strong in large part because nobody believes that America would ever default on its debt. Yet in 1933, Franklin D. Roosevelt did just that, when in a bid to pull the country out of depression, he depreciated the U.S. dollar in relation to gold, effectively annulling all debt contracts. It began on April 5, 1933, when FDR ordered Americans to sell all their gold holdings to the government. This was followed by the abandonment of the gold standard, the unilateral and retroactive rewriting of contracts, and the devaluation of the dollar. Anyone who held public and private debt suddenly saw its value reduced by nearly half, and debtors—including the U.S. government—suddenly owed their creditors far less . . . The banks fought back, and a bitter battle for gold ensued.

By any measure, FDR's steps were drastic, but these were desperate times.

Years later, early in the Second World War, when FDR's friend and "opposite number," Winston Churchill, became prime minister, things looked close to hopeless. The seemingly invincible Nazi war machine was steamrolling across Europe, and Britain was next on the hit list. But Churchill, through force of will, kept up public morale despite one disaster after another: the fall of France; the retreat and evacuation from Dunkirk; the Blitz that bombed out London and other British cities; and, after Japan's attack on Pearl Harbor, the humiliating capture and capitulation of Hong Kong and "fortress Singapore." Amid this, German U-boats were sinking cargo ships at a rate that brought the UK close to starvation.

A lesser leader might have sought a face-saving peace deal with Berlin. Churchill's now famous "we shall fight on the beaches" speech to the House of Commons after defeat in Dunkirk made it clear that he would do no such thing. His indomitable personal leadership kept up spirits until the tide of the war could be turned. FDR helped, too, by making wartime America the world's "arsenal of democracy," with factories running around the clock to supply the US, Britain, and their allies.

Today we lionize these larger-than-life leaders who parted the proverbial Red Sea of their day. But it's worth noting that neither Franklin Roosevelt nor Winston Churchill took office with broad public support or universal public confidence in their ability to succeed. To the contrary, the elites of the day worried that the deck was stacked against men they regarded as untested, mediocre leaders, and questioned their fitness for the Herculean tasks of winning a war, restoring peace, and unleashing the power of economic reconstruction with public support.

Both came from wealthy, historically prominent families, one a distant (fifth) cousin of President Teddy Roosevelt, the other a direct descendant of early-1700s English war hero John Churchill, honored by being made the first duke of Marlborough. FDR, a patrician Harvard man afflicted with a paralytic illness generally thought to be polio, did not seem the obvious choice to lead the country and the world. When he took office, the left called him a fascist, the right believed he was a social-ist and a "traitor to his class," and many others simply thought he had a dictatorial streak. His wife, Eleanor, a distant cousin, was also controver-sial due to her active involvement in politics and support for progressive causes at the time such as civil rights and labor protections. FDR proved all of the naysayers wrong.

Churchill, an undisciplined and poor student in his youth, never made it to university and was widely regarded as a reckless, heavy-drinking dilettante who tried his hand successively at the army, journal-ism, and politics, including changing parties. No wonder the period in his life from 1929 to 1939 is often referred to as his "wilderness years," a time when most of his contemporaries had already written him off. He, too, proved the naysayers wrong.

Churchill helped win the war, but Britain's equivalent of America's New Deal came only *after* the war, as the troops returned home with expectations of improved living standards in "a country fit for heroes." Despite severe budget strains and the continuation of food rationing, the UK's iconic National Health Service, today a much-loved institution of national pride, was launched in 1948 to provide free universal healthcare. Other New Deal–type programs were rolled out, including National Insurance, the British analogue of America's Social Security, and Great Britain's first universal, tuition-free secondary education.

Meanwhile, postwar Continental Europe was a smoldering ruin in 1945, and even such victors as France were financially bankrupted by the war. The far-sighted Marshall Plan sped recovery in Western Europe to such a degree that many older people look upon the period that followed the war as a golden age of economic growth, good jobs, and a new sense of optimism.

Of course, many hurdles had to be overcome. Italy, for example, had experienced so many convulsions under Fascism and through the war that many ordinary people were both weary and skeptical. There was actually a trend in the immediate postwar period called *qualunquismo*—in effect, people choosing apathy and indifference since "all politicians are crooks," "all journalists lie," and there seemed little that anyone could do about it. Unfortunately, that very same "nothing will ever change" attitude has taken hold in a sizable slice of our society today. What's worse, we not only have a lack of public confidence in the competence of government, but also a much more pernicious false narrative about a "deep state" subverting government to meet the needs of a corrupt group of nefarious elite officials at the public's expense. Politicians have continually used the public's distrust of the state to their advantage, positioning themselves as victims of deep-rooted conspiracies. It's a dangerous and absolutely false perception propagated by those, at home and abroad, who seek to do the very thing of which they accuse the deep state. The 2020 election has afforded us a chance to leave these ideas behind and start a new national conversation based on mutual respect and trust in our institutions.

As for Europe, postwar Italy was able to get out of its funk and shake off its pessimism, and in 1957 the stylish yet affordable Fiat 500 ("*Cinquecento*") city car came to symbolize the country's industrial and consumer resurgence, even as governments in Rome continued to come and go. The French call that period *Les Trentes Glorieuses* ("the 30 glorious years," from 1945 to 1975), while Germans still speak proudly of their economic miracle of the same period, the *Wirtschaftswunder*. Those were of course quite good years for the United States, too. Rising prosperity even invented the phenomenon of the teenager, as before this period teens didn't have much free time or spending money and often had to start working as young as 16, if not earlier, to help support themselves and their families. Instead, more young adults—young and poor—could go to college and explore different career paths, buy houses and property, and live comfortable lives—the American Dream.

Unsurprisingly, previous generations, including Baby Boomers, believed fervently in "progress." Many such notions of what the future would look like were of course not necessarily realistic, coming as they did from sources as diverse and ephemeral as World's Fairs, science fiction, and the Space Program.

But a belief in progress itself was realistic—after all, the 20th century offered a cavalcade of life improvements, ranging from refrigeration and air conditioning to antibiotics and commercial jet travel. Improvements in quality of life, widely distributed, were palpable. People felt that they contributed to and benefited from these advances. However, progress is not, and has never been, a straight-line process; rather, it happens in fits and starts, with steps backward at times.

What the last century can tell us is not to be too quick to bet against progress. We have a historic opportunity to transform our recent breakdowns into national and even global breakthroughs. History will rightly hold us accountable if we don't seize the moment.

For those worried that expanding the power and reach of governments is a slippery and dangerous slope, history, again, is a good teacher. Josef Joffe—editor-publisher of Germany's influential *Die Zeit* newspaper and Stanford fellow—had this to say during the height of the COVID-19 lockdown:

> In short, national emergencies in the West do not breed despots . . . Predicting an authoritarian takeover, the merchants of angst ignore critical points. First, the liberal state gives far more than it grabs. In sharp contrast with the 1930s, when mass misery fueled the rise of tyrants, the Western welfare state delivers trillions in cash and liquidity to ease the pain and safeguard the economy's future . . . Second, the so-called security state does not wear jackboots. It is armed not with bayonets, but with the consent of the governed, which is another word for "legitimacy." Thus . . . 93 percent of Germans approve[d] of the partial lock-down. Three out of four Canadians approve[d] the government's handling of the crisis . . . Third, manifest trust does not deliver a blank check, and the elected know it.

Of course, the Trump administration's controversial deployment of federal forces in full combat gear in Portland, Oregon, and other US cities in response to mass Black Lives Matter protests prompted many to worry we might well be on the slippery slope to martial law. However, Joffe's main points still hold across the developed world, even if "jack-boots" were indeed seen on American city streets during 2020 in a disconcerting haze of tear gas and flash-bang grenades. I emphatically do not believe that this kind of heavy-handed militarized response to protests will ever become the new normal for the United States. It's been an aberration, and I hope a temporary one—just look at how much outrage the militarized responses provoked among much of American society. At the same time, who can forget the spectacle of Joe Biden's inauguration with 25,000 National Guard troops and thousands of other law enforcement officials summoned to secure the event and ensure the peaceful transfer of power? But this, too, will pass. I am old enough to remember walking to work in downtown Washington, DC, in 1972, with tanks and troops deployed in most major city circles, with gun and tank barrels pointedly intended to intimidate antiwar protesters. Then they were gone, as was the president who deployed them.

Speaking of aberrations, while we can't expect greatness or brilliance from every American president, we must absolutely insist that our head of state and government be someone of sound moral character, good judgment, and an acceptable degree of wisdom and common sense. This is not just because the US president has his or her finger on the proverbial nuclear button. Presidential powers are vast, involving everything from initiating major legislative prescriptions to establishing and funding government programs, addressing the basic health and well-being of the country's citizens, making appointments to the federal judiciary—including nominating Supreme Court justices—foreign policy, and tax and economic policy. The president also appoints some 4,000 high-level officials who will implement government policy and make crucial decisions with wide-ranging implications. But there's actually even more to those wide-ranging powers, and very likely the following will surprise and alarm you.

Very few Americans are aware of the 50 to 60 highly classified "Presidential Emergency Action Documents" that give the president almost unlimited near-dictatorial powers during emergencies. None have ever been invoked to date, nor has the public ever been allowed to see their contents, and no portion has ever been leaked—such is their secrecy. They were enacted "to implement extraordinary presidential authority in response to extraordinary situations," according to the Brennan Center at NYU Law School. Some may reasonably question the constitutionality of all this, which began with the Eisenhower administration's efforts to create the basis for "continuity of government" in the event of a Soviet nuclear attack. Yet these secret executive powers, if abused or misused, could put our lives and liberties in grave danger. If it wasn't already obvious before, it should be now: only a leader of impeccable character should ever be allowed to occupy the Oval Office. The policy community must consider this closely given how close we came during the Trump presidency to the complete breakdown of the responsible exercise of power. Do we have sufficient checks and balances in our system to effectively deal with any future president who might not be willing or able to "preserve, protect and defend the Constitution of the United States"?

In the post-Trump era, it is not surprising that even more Americans see their government as an ineffectual mess and a roadblock to innovation, though it is important to note that this attitude is a relatively recent phenomenon. Even in the aftermath of the Watergate scandal, Jimmy Carter was elected to restore confidence in the "integrity" of government—rather than its competence as such. It is true that Ronald Reagan famously (or infamously) said, "Government is not the solution to our problem, government is the problem." But history shows us that with the right leadership, ideas, and strategic and effective use of resources, the US government in its many manifestations can be a tremendously innovative force, generating positive economic and technological ripple effects throughout the economy and society.

A quick focus on some of government's more unheralded contributions to the quality of life and livelihood for many Americans will offer a high note on which to conclude this chapter. Some of the astonishing ways in which the US government has actually enabled many quantum leaps range from the development of the internet and the LED to the CAT scan and computer mouse—ingenious spinoffs from work done in the Space Program, the Defense Department, and other agencies. Most of us associate the National Aeronautics and Space Administration (NASA) with key events like the first moon landing—an astounding achievement in and of itself—and subsequent Apollo and Space Shuttle missions. That's all well and good, but that's just the tip of the iceberg.

Instead of thinking of space exploration as an expensive, totally disconnected activity that pays no dividends to our earthly economy, we should remind ourselves that many things we take for granted today, like camera phones, water purification systems, handheld vacuums, wireless headphones, and scratch-resistant lenses, were initially produced to meet astronauts' needs while high above earth. Instead of "Houston, we have a problem," we really should be saying, "Houston, we have a solution." We should not forget, too, that NASA still pioneers innovation in space travel today, which very much includes robotics. The robots we've sent into space, from the Explorer 1 satellite in 1958 to the Mars 2020 *Perseverance* rover of today, have been designed and produced out of NASA's world-famous Jet Propulsion Laboratory, based at the California Institute of Technology in the Los Angeles area.

And how many people know that the internet was born from a US Department of Defense effort to improve communication between units, led by its Advanced Research Projects Agency? Now known as the Defense Advanced Research Projects Agency (DARPA), its research and development achievements go much further than hatching the internet, as if that weren't enough. Every time you turn on Google Maps or use your phone's location services, you're benefiting from DARPA's work on the Global Positioning System (GPS). Unsurprisingly, DARPA remains at the cutting edge in areas as diverse as quantum computing, "deep" machine learning algorithms, and data privacy and security. As one analyst explains, DARPA's "mission is to anticipate, prevent, and create technological surprise." The value created by DARPA has been so great that the United Kingdom wants a "DARPA" of its own, and in 2020 earmarked £800 million to launch a similar "blue sky" research agency from scratch.

And who remembers this: back in the 1990s, two Stanford graduate students started working on an internet search engine using $4.5 million of federal research money from NASA, DARPA, and the National Science Foundation (NSF). Their names are Larry Page and Sergey Brin, and the rest is history, as they say—what young person can imagine a world without Google? Similarly, DARPA funded numerous efforts to research speech recognition, starting back in the 1950s. Some $150 million went to SRI International, where I spent a formative decade of my career. Originally known as the Stanford Research Institute, it was spun off from Stanford University in 1970. SRI International was also at the origins of something called "Siri." Apple bought Siri from SRI in 2010 and now uses its speech recognition technology on its devices. Speaking of speech, are you someone who always watches TV with the subtitles on? You can thank employees at what was then called the National Bureau of Standards in the 1970s for launching closed captioning. And if you like your iPhone's touch screen, you should look up the Established Program to Stimulate Competitive Research, an NSF initiative that funded touch screen research at the University of Delaware.

All these examples show the extraordinary power, ingenuity, and economic benefit of government-led basic research, when it's well funded and properly directed. Once upon a time there were companies with the long-term vision and ability to fund similar research efforts, but those days are mostly gone. During the 20th century, AT&T's Bell Labs was a marvel dubbed the "idea factory"—nine Nobel Prizes are associated with Bell Labs, and their roll call of extraordinary inventions is long, not least among them the transistor and the laser.

Sadly, few corporations today feel they can justify such long-range research efforts with uncertain long-term payoffs. Peter Thiel, cofounder of PayPal and Facebook's first investor, decries the narrowness and "short-termism" of Silicon Valley today, despite the notion that venture capital is supposed to take the long view and open up new frontiers.

One of his well-known lines is, "We wanted flying cars, instead we got 140 characters," a reference to the creation of Twitter. Clearly there are things that only the government can do, and when it does them well, the return on investment can astonish even Wall Street. But this is a fact many have forgotten or never learned, which is another reason why I say, "Study history."

Somehow we have lost sight of government's important catalyzing role, both in scientific innovation and in helping a nation recover from profound shocks. I recall back in the early 1990s, as Russia was adjusting to a post-Soviet system of private enterprise, having the opportunity to discuss this transition in Moscow with Anatoly Chubais, then head of the newly formed Russian Privatization Agency. As I was pointing out how the government must play a role in enhancing competitiveness and funding basic research, Chubais stopped me and said, "Oh, you don't understand, this is no longer the Soviet Union. We are now pursuing a capitalist development model and government has no role. This is a laissez-faire system in which the fittest private sector survivors run the show." I replied, "With all due respect, Minister Chubais, there is no successful capitalist system in the world in which government doesn't play a role. The key question is not *whether* government has a role to play, but rather what is the appropriate role that government must play." And these are precisely the kinds of questions guiding the initial, highly ambitious goals and proposals of the Biden administration, evident from its day-one initiatives, as it seeks to restore trust in government's ability to meet the critical needs of a deeply challenged society.

We still have much to learn from FDR and Churchill, great leaders who faced the horrors of
the Great Depression and the Second World War
and inspired a frightened public to overcome the
odds and achieve victory. In this meeting in 1941
off the coast of Newfoundland, they signed the
Atlantic Charter, a precursor to the UN Charter
that laid the foundation for the sustained peace
and prosperity of the post-war global order.

CHAPTER FOUR

GREAT LEADERS CHANGE REALITY

"A genuine leader is not a searcher
for consensus but a molder of consensus."
—MARTIN LUTHER KING, JR.

"If your actions inspire others to dream more,
learn more, do more and become more,
you are a leader."
—*ATTRIBUTED TO* JOHN QUINCY ADAMS

"Management is doing things right,
leadership is doing the right things."
—PETER DRUCKER

The old cynical joke that people get the leaders they deserve . . . is actually not very funny, especially given what we've experienced in recent years. In many places, people have gotten worse than they deserve, or at least worse than what they needed. Perhaps that would help explain why, with the rise of populist leaders and their snake oil propositions in this century, we've seen increased use of the esoteric word "kakistocracy," defined as "a state or society governed by its least suitable or competent citizens."

It's tough to imagine this term having much currency in the era of FDR and Churchill. Whether it was FDR as the antidote to the Great Depression or Churchill in besieged World War II Britain—or countless other examples—great leaders go beyond inspiring people, shaping moods, and galvanizing public support—they can actually change outcomes, delivering a future different from current realities. Personal resilience and character matter. As George Kennan, the American diplomat and one of the "wise men" of US postwar foreign policy, wrote to then Secretary of State Dean Acheson during a low point in the Korean War, "In international, as in private life what counts most is not really what happens to someone but how he bears what happens to him." All the more true for those in positions of power today.

And when great leaders don't emerge naturally, mass social movements born of frustration often burst onto the scene, which themselves generate new leaders. The old saying "Cometh the hour, cometh the man" still has a ring of truth, though today, of course, the powerful leader who emerges in a crisis could just as easily be a woman. The UK in the 1970s was a basket case approaching Third World status, and out of that mess came the "Iron Lady"—Margaret Thatcher—a still-controversial figure who nonetheless proves the point. Since then, many of the world's most celebrated leaders have been women, including longtime German chancellor Angela Merkel and New Zealand's admired and effective prime minister Jacinda Ardern. Grave situations combined with poor leadership often create the popular groundswell needed to coax out both good leaders who can do the job and the leadership skills needed to get it done.

This is no less true in the corporate world, where a great CEO can turn around a firm that everyone has written off, or develop and execute an audacious new vision for a company in need of transformation. Steve Jobs of Apple was sometimes criticized for his so-called reality distortion field: his determination to create the seemingly impossible. But it was possible, and so we have the iPhone—mundane now, but a miracle when first launched. The lack of such visionary leadership can have the opposite effect. Take the case of Nokia. With the launch of the 2100-series handheld in 1994, the company was able to surge to become the world leader in mobile phones by 1998. By 2005, the company had sold one billion phones and appeared unstoppable. Yet just two short years later, Steve Jobs's vision of the iPhone was realized. In 2008, Nokia reported a 30-percent drop in profits while Apple reported one of its most successful years ever, which then-CEO Steve Jobs attributed to the rapid growth of the iPhone. When Nokia CEO Stephen Elop declared in 2011 that the company "was standing on a burning platform," he saw the writing on the wall. By 2013, the company's handset division was acquired by Microsoft for a small fraction of its former worth. History is replete with many such examples. The failure to anticipate and effectively respond to change—even when it is upon you—can be deadly. Capable, visionary leadership matters.

To those young people who believe the cards are stacked against them because they lack elite credentials or family money, longtime Coca-Cola chairman and CEO Muhtar Kent would be happy to remind them that he got his start by answering a classified ad and learning the business from the back of a Coke delivery truck. Muhtar told me of his first year at Coca-Cola, delivering this quintessentially American product to retailers in the backwaters of rural America: "Get up at 3 AM, load up the trucks, and go into the market." It turned out to be a fantastic, if less than glamorous, learning experience at the beginning of his career. Muhtar later went on to "deliver" at Coke what may well be the most fundamental transformation of a corporate icon in American history. One of Muhtar's maxims for success in life and indeed in any field is "Never eat alone," as one should use every opportunity to create and build personal relationships. During the pandemic, when normal patterns of life (and travel) were completely disrupted, he advised people to stay closely engaged (even if electronically) with their existing "bank" of valuable relationships.

As a philanthropist, Muhtar has also put his money where he passionately believes it can do the most good: the new Kent Global Leadership Program on Conflict Resolution at Columbia University in New

York. As he told me recently, "It started with a fundamental belief that large political, social issues, problems, challenges around the world can only be solved by the coming together of . . . government, business, and civil society. In other words, government alone can't solve the big health, economic, social, political, [and] geopolitical issues of the world. Business cannot certainly do it alone. And civil society, education, universities, NGOs, et cetera, can't do it alone. But if you bring these three together, in what I call the Golden Triangle, then there's a chance that some of these big societal, big political, big geopolitical issues can be solved, at least partially."

Another example of a great corporate leader is Sir Rod Eddington, who was a truly transformational CEO at both British Airways and Cathay Pacific. Rod wasn't exactly born to elite circumstances: he grew up in the harsh bush of Western Australia and never saw a TV until he was ten or eleven years old. Once a very bright young cricket star who won a Rhodes Scholarship to Oxford, Rod likes to say, "Never stop learning. I take good ideas wherever I find them." I wholeheartedly agree.

Sir Rod's compatriot, Catherine Livingstone, chair of the Commonwealth Bank of Australia, has done her own bit to add to the leadership lexicon with her "green arrow principle," based on her childhood experience with Australia's traffic lights. Instead of seeing a "red light" in business, life, or politics as a dead end or long delay, Catherine learned that the indirect, alternate route of following the green turn arrows that can accompany red lights can actually get you to your destination faster than the more direct, but sometimes impeded, straightforward path. What may seem a rather obvious insight is actually a critical "never-say-no" approach to finding alternative routes to your goals. Later in this book, when I describe America's best-case future and the 10 propositions we need to focus on to succeed, I'll readily admit that, while a much brighter future is possible and indeed very doable, we will have to overcome setbacks and blockages and reroute as necessary. To paraphrase the words of the late, great management guru Peter Drucker, to reach our destination, we sometimes have to improvise.

Likewise, in South Asia, Mukesh Ambani, India's richest man (and one of Asia's richest), could be taking it easy, but instead he's working furiously to bring inexpensive digital connectivity and basic financial and other services to up to a billion poor people, many without running water or electricity. I have seen up close the tenacity and courage of this soft-spoken and understated titan, who has had the vision and audacity to invest more than $30 billion of his own money (despite the skepticism of many "experts") to bring digital connections to nearly 20 percent of the world's currently unconnected and unbanked people. This may go down as one of history's most courageous and visionary investments. And now Mukesh has his sights on building the Indian equivalent of Apple, Amazon, and Google—all in one integrated enterprise.

Are these incredible stories mere nostalgic vestiges of a bygone era of expansive opportunity, or is there some pay-it-forward truth from which tomorrow's leaders can glean inspiration, hope, and direction in the midst of so much dislocation, uncertainty, and despair?

Leadership matters, and the lives of leaders—past and present—offer important lessons to a world and its office holders seemingly mired in insurmountable problems. Vision and direction are key to leadership in an otherwise confused and troubled world. As Henry Kissinger said in an apparent echo of Yogi Berra, "If you don't know where you're going, every road will get you nowhere." Well, unless we know the kind of leaders we need, we won't be able to find them.

Many people now believe that only the ruthless and nasty seem to get ahead, and that so-called leaders are often self-obsessed, "looking out for #1" bullies. American-born and UK-based polymath David Bodanis has studied what kind of leadership styles succeed over the long haul, and the title of his latest book hints at the answer: *The Art of Fairness: The Power of Decency in a World Turned Mean*. As *The Economist* summed it up, "Ruling by fear may work for a while, but it is doomed to fail in the long run." Bodanis even gives the example of the man who coined the phrase "nice guys finish last"—legendary but often unpleasant baseball manager Leo Durocher. For all his tough talk, questionable behavior, and sharp elbows, Durocher himself finished last. In fact, fundamental decency, courtesy, and fairness are great assets in any leader, not signs of weakness as is so often assumed. Even Donald Trump's willingness to put "winning" ahead of principle couldn't concoct a 2020 reelection victory, no matter how many accomplices he managed to recruit in his extraordinary attempt to subvert the will of the electorate.

Of course, the best leaders aren't born, or even made—they're forged in crucibles that push them to their limits and beyond. The Abraham Lincoln we remember today didn't start out as the Abe Lincoln of legend. Read Ted Widmer's recent book *Lincoln on the Verge: Thirteen Days to Washington* to see what I mean. Widmer tells the evocative story of the exhausting and perilous 13-day train journey that Lincoln—who was not universally popular and whose leadership qualities remained untested—took in February 1861 from Illinois to Washington for his inauguration, when the United States was on the brink of disintegrating and probably the most divided it has been and ever will be. Lincoln made several planned stops along the way and survived at least two assassination attempts during the journey. He arrived in Washington a taller man—I'm not speaking of his height—and a leader better prepared for the much more harrowing trials to come, with the Civil War just around the corner. It's a dose of inspiration for those who are looking for insights into how great leadership evolves, with its practitioners often hiding in plain sight.

As renowned presidential historian and leadership expert Doris Kearns Goodwin has studied, written, and spoken about, great leaders tested in crisis come out stronger, as they show empathy, resilience in the face of adversity, personal humility, trustworthiness, an ambition bigger than themselves focused on the greater good, optimism, and a unifying spirit that helps them lead the way out of tough circumstances.

I'm no Abe Lincoln, to be sure, but I'd like to share with you the story of my own trial by fire as a corporate leader. In 2006, my fellow partners elected me managing partner and chairman of Kearney, one of the world's largest and oldest global management-consulting firms. This was shortly after our management buyout had returned our firm to the more natural state of partner ownership after a tortuous 10 years as a corporate subsidiary of Electronic Data Systems (EDS) (H. Ross Perot's once high-flying, now defunct, data management and outsourcing giant, the remnants of which got absorbed into Hewlett-Packard).

Our firm had spun out of control in the last few years of that uneasy marriage (which had followed 70 very successful years as a private global partnership). The firm we partners bought back was in bad shape, having lost key clients, talent, and most importantly, vision and a sense of purpose. We were, in the words of Morgan Stanley, a firm "on chemotherapy and life support." And as partner-owners, having dug deep into our own pockets to buy back our troubled firm, we were surely apprehensive about its prospects.

But it was very clear to me that before we could rebuild our trusted relationships with key stakeholders, we needed to ground ourselves in the principles that had helped define uniquely who we were and what our value proposition was to our people and our clients. We had become Balkanized, and we had to shift from what had drifted toward an "eat what you kill" warlord culture back to our previously collegial "one-firm firm" global orientation.

So, I began with global, firm-wide town hall meetings in which my leadership team and I articulated our distinctive Kearney vision and principles, in hopes of starting a prairie fire among our younger consultants. We reconnected to founder Tom Kearney's values of "essential rightness" and aligned around a new statement, which we gave to every employee on a small laminated card that I urged them to carry as a constant reminder: "By doing good, we will do well for our clients, ourselves, and our community. We do this with passion for people, ideas, and the world in which we live."

To many of my hard-boiled, bottom-line-focused colleagues in the firm, this seemed like idealistic fluff. To me, however, and especially to our younger talent, this was at the core of our value proposition: to make a positive difference in the world by making a positive difference for our clients and the communities in which we serve. To put some flesh on the bone, I asked my fellow partners to dig deeper into their pockets to fund investments in the development of our people and our communities through various kinds of pro bono services. And what's more, I pledged that our firm would be the first global consulting firm to become carbon neutral. Needless to say, these measures were not very popular with many understandably anxious partners seeking—and needing—to restart the firm's financial performance engine.

Happily, in relatively short order, the results—restored relationships, fast-growing revenues, much higher morale, and a repaired reputation— were amazing, as was our ability to become the first management consulting firm to achieve carbon neutrality. Despite having been dealt the difficult hand of the Great Recession midstream in our firm-rebuilding effort, we achieved a phoenix-from-the-ashes turnaround by reaffirming the principles on which the firm was founded. Tom Kearney, one of management consulting's earliest and greatest pioneers, would have been pleased not only with the firm's return to worldly success, but especially with our fidelity to his and our highest values. His credo is prominently proclaimed at the entrance to every Kearney office: "Our success as consultants will depend on the essential rightness of the advice we give and our capacity for convincing those in authority that it is good."

Being a leader, or indeed having any role in management consulting, means being on a plane constantly, at least in normal times. The obvious downside is having to be away from home and family so often, while the upside is being exposed to what's happening in and around the world, literally first hand, and seeing new trends before they get noticed elsewhere. And this sense of serendipity is often a pleasant, unexpected bonus. Perhaps if you fly a sufficient number of millions of miles, you bump into anyone and everyone—or at least that's how it seemed to work out for me. My travel surprises have included being seated next to Stevie Wonder on a flight to Nigeria, running into Morgan Fairchild, Sting, Yul Brynner, Julie Andrews, George Clooney, Ringo Starr, and Queen Latifah while globe-trotting, and having a front row seat at the filming of *The Godfather Part III* while in Sicily exploring my family roots.

This is all a way of saying that leaders—and indeed anyone who aspires to succeed—who are content to simply sit behind a desk and make Zoom calls (even though that's a public health necessity in a pandemic) or reside within an ivory tower and remain unaware of what's happening on the ground will miss out on being exposed to unique and enriching experiences and points of view. As Canadian thinker and futurist Marshall McLuhan once said, a point of view is no substitute for real insight into what's going on. This applies to those at the very top of the corporate ladder just as much as it does to those referred to in *Hamilton* as the "young, scrappy, and hungry" just starting out. So, when it's possible, get on a plane, preferably to some country or place you've never been to before. Do something different. Widen your lens, and take it all in. No matter your position or professional experience, you will learn something new. You won't learn anything new breathing your own exhaust. Leadership, and in fact any kind of real success, requires depth and breadth of diverse experiences, now more than ever.

When I had the opportunity to ask Alan Joyce, the CEO who successfully turned Qantas Airways into one of the world's most respected and customer-acclaimed airlines, to what he attributed his success, he quickly observed that having broad and diverse insights from a team with various backgrounds and experiences was critical. "One of the things I look for in good leaders is people who can—excuse the airline analogy—operate most of the time at 35,000 feet." He recounted one example of how instrumental diverse team input was to his decision-making, even under the most difficult of circumstances. He shared with me the harrowing story of when a Qantas flight in 2010 (QF32, an Airbus super-jumbo A380 going from Heathrow to Sydney with a stop at Singapore Changi) encountered a potentially catastrophic uncontained engine failure. He recounted how a diverse and inclusive group, including his chief engineer, each bringing their unique experiences to bear, was quickly able to ascertain the nature of the problem. Not only was the plane brought to the ground safely, thanks to live team and technical input and audacious piloting skills, but also the group was able to agree unanimously to ground the A380 fleet at once—just as three other A380s were preparing to take off, sparing the prospect of a very grim air disaster. No wonder Qantas is regarded as the world's safest airline, having never had a fatality since the dawn of the jet age some seven decades ago.

My point is that great leaders can and do change the course of history. From leading politicians to corporate executives to visionary inventors, top talent often emerges to meet the challenges and seize the opportunities of the time, and I am convinced it will continue to do so. What's more, history has shown again and again that even those not in leadership positions can—and often do—step up and work toward a collective goal. What would FDR and Churchill have been able to achieve, for instance, without the support of normal, everyday citizens helping the war effort in whatever way they could—including the young men who served on the front lines in World War II, the wives who did the jobs their husbands had left behind, or the millions of ordinary people who simply kept calm and carried on, making the sacrifices a successful war effort required? Today's world, as we're all painfully aware, is not short of challenges, from pernicious inequality to climate change and many other colliding crises that can leave us feeling demoralized or hopeless. However, I believe that rough times like those we've experienced have produced some of humanity's best leaders. As I'll talk about in the next chapter, even societies that feel like they're coming unglued can build consensus and come roaring back—often thanks to savvy and visionary leaders and their motivated followers.

America in the 1960s was increasingly a divided country, but the Space Program inspired and brought together the nation. In February 1962 at Cape Canaveral, even President Kennedy seemed in awe of John Glenn's Friendship 7 Mercury capsule that made the world's first ever orbital manned flight.

CHAPTER FIVE

EVEN FRAGMENTED SOCIETIES CAN BUILD CONSENSUS AROUND BIG GOALS

"The only thing necessary for the triumph
of evil is for good men to do nothing."
—*ATTRIBUTED TO* **EDMUND BURKE**

"In matters of style, swim with the current;
in matters of principle, stand like a rock."
—*ATTRIBUTED TO* **THOMAS JEFFERSON**

"Take calculated risks.
That is quite different from being rash."
—**GEORGE PATTON**

Our formerly broad-based common culture, built on a strong social fabric, a robust civil society, and a high degree of shared values and experiences, reinforced by a concentrated, widely trusted mass media (e.g., CBS, NBC, ABC, *Time* and *LIFE* magazines, etc.) simply isn't coming back, at least not as we boomers once knew it.

Not many people spend their evenings in community service clubs, fraternal societies, or other local groups anymore, as Robert D. Putnam, author of the best-selling book *Bowling Alone*, has powerfully reminded us. For example, are you yourself spending your free evenings and weekends with the Lions, Kiwanis, Elks, Masons, Knights of Columbus, or the like? I didn't think so. If you're like many people, just before the coronavirus pandemic you might have been devoting less time to family and your circle of friends than to your smartphone, computer, or tablet, "liking" photos and social media posts online, watching YouTube videos, or viewing a show or movie on a streaming service.

Most societies are now too diverse, fractious, and "siloed" to make a common culture possible, even in relatively homogenous countries, never mind such incredibly heterogeneous ones as the US. And our reliance on social media in lieu of in-person friendships is contributing to rising rates of loneliness, especially in young people. One 2020 Cigna study found that over 70 percent of American workers ages 18 to 22 reported sometimes or always feeling lonely. This may seem counterintuitive given that so many of today's young people engage with others on TikTok, Instagram, and other social media apps, with some even making careers on those platforms. And yet, these apps seem to be doing little to help create a sense of common culture or belonging.

It is puzzling that even though technology can help us seem more connected with each other than ever, what we're getting instead is more loneliness. That's because loneliness is not about how many friends you have or how big your family is. It's a feeling of being disconnected from others, the world at large, and even material gains. Lonely people feel that they have no voice and are immaterial to society at large. As the author, economist, and academic Noreena Hertz wrote in the *Financial Times*, "This combination of personal and political isolation helps to explain not only why levels of loneliness are so high globally today, but also why loneliness and politics have in recent years become so closely linked."

Loneliness should concern more than just the parents of teen TikTok users. Loneliness is not only linked with poor economic productivity and higher workplace absenteeism. Emerging research shows that lonely individuals are also more likely to perceive others with suspicion. In one 2019 British study from King's College London, lonely youth aged 12 to 18 were asked to describe their neighborhood, and their siblings who did not report feeling lonely were asked to do the same. The lonely children by and large said that their neighborhoods were less socially cohesive than their siblings did. This means that lonely individuals may be more likely to view the world—and other individuals—with distrust. Noreena Hertz argues that populists have played on this sense of detachment and distrust for political gain. "By reinforcing their followers' sense of abandonment and marginalization and setting this against an apparent political favoring of people unlike them—typically immigrants and sometimes simply people of a different religion or color—populists' fear-mongering revs up emotions, anxiety, and insecurity and manipulates ethnic and religious difference to garner allegiance and support," she writes.

While daunting, all of that shouldn't stop us—or good leaders—from building new consensus around critical issues and big, motivational (yet realistically achievable) public goals that spark the imagination of people in all stations of life. The American psyche needs a booster shot of can-do optimism that comes from pragmatic, get-it-done ingenuity, animated by leaders who can inspire the best in us. This can-do behavior has been a unique character trait that has driven American exceptionalism against all odds since the inception of this republic.

I recall vividly a discussion I had back in the recession of the early '90s with a French CEO who had come to the US to announce the closing of their American plant. He was shaking his head at how fundamentally different the reaction was among American workers confronted with such news from the kinds of reactions he had grown accustomed to from having to shutter failing French factories. In France, he said, an announcement of this kind prompts instant protest and vociferous, angry opposition. "The US reaction couldn't be more different, with management and rank and file labor wanting to work together to help solve the problem. 'What can we do to turn this around? Can we work longer hours, find ways to improve our product, cut costs?'" was the American response. There has always been this American pragmatic sense of finding the ways and means to *solve* the problem, to change reality, rather than simply accepting a negative outcome.

Even during the challenges of the coronavirus, Americans remained pragmatic and inventive. None exemplify our country's ability to remain creative in the face of crisis better than Dr. Jennifer Doudna, a distinguished biochemist and co-discoverer of the revolutionary CRISPR gene editing technology. Her work has contributed to a "CRISPR revolution," and her research on genome editing ultimately won her the Nobel Prize for Chemistry in 2020. When she and I talked about the potential of these technologies to help manage the coronavirus during April 2020, Jennifer said, "We really need scientists from all stripes to step up right now and take whatever expertise they have, whatever tools they have, whatever research approaches they're using for things that are maybe completely unrelated to coronavirus, and bring them to bear on this current pandemic." Professionals of differing backgrounds needed to work together to come up with solutions, Jennifer explained, so as to not only manage the crisis at hand but also prepare better for new challenges on the horizon: "The more we can do to both understand the biology of this virus and its transmission, but also to really think about how we prepare as a country and globally to get ready for the next coronavirus or anything else that comes along in the future, I think will be critical." That's the kind of innovative can-do spirit that led to the development of COVID-19 vaccines in months, rather than the decades we have had to wait for effective vaccine development in the past.

Of course, the business world has its own ambitious leaders that look to solve today's challenges while building a better world for future generations as well. Pioneering entrepreneurs such as Jeff Bezos and Elon Musk have been personally inspired by the idea of human colonization of space, and in the case of Bezos, of the entire cosmos. As private citizens they are free, of course, to spend their own money on such initiatives. However, this kind of goal isn't what I have in mind. We can build new consensus around a compelling vision and dream big dreams, but those motivational goals, though ambitious, have to be achievable and down to earth (if you'll excuse the pun), promising real benefits to those who embrace the vision and help enable it. Reaching for extraterrestrial opportunities won't help all of us who are gravitationally tied to a failing planet earth, no matter what spin-off benefits ultimately might emerge from a new push into space. Interestingly and unsurprisingly, many others in the "private-jet class" are more interested in *terrestrial* escape plans and have bought safe-haven properties in New Zealand, and in some cases, like Peter Thiel, have even become New Zealand citizens, since nationals of a country can't be turned away at the border even during pandemics or other world-crisis conditions.

But that's the difference between the small and rich "mobile minority" and the vast "immobile majority," who have to make the best of the place and circumstances in which they live. Some commentators speculate that COVID-19 created a new sense of solidarity in many societies—what the Brits like to call "the Blitz spirit"—symbolized, elsewhere in Europe, by those in Italy and Spain who took to their balconies to sing together and toast one another in the evenings amid draconian shelter-in-place measures. Is this the "new nationalism" that Teddy Roosevelt talked about back in Kansas in 1910, where citizens "put the national need before the sectional or personal advantage"? We can only hope, since such attitudes seem to benefit the individual as well as society at large. While sheltering in place proved incredibly difficult for many, a study by the American Psychological Association notes that such programs have actually helped *decrease* feelings of social isolation in cases when neighbors banded together, helped one another, and worked toward a common goal: surviving the virus.

Other equally well-informed analysts say this is balderdash—that the pandemic will in fact ultimately reinforce the polarizing, us-versus-them, close-the-border mentality that was already well entrenched. If a new spirit of solidarity is rising, great—but many simply do not see it.

Even some of today's brightest minds, like Pulitzer Prize–winning author and top journalist Anne Applebaum, find themselves uncharacteristically unsure or perplexed about what comes next. In her 2020 book *Twilight of Democracy: The Seductive Lure of Authoritarianism,* Anne writes about our situation as she perceives it: "It might be a turning point . . . We may be doomed, like glittering, multiethnic Habsburg Vienna or creative, decadent Weimar Berlin, to be swept away into irrelevance. It is possible we are already living through the twilight of democracy; that our civilization may already be heading for anarchy or tyranny, as the ancient philosophers and America's founders once feared . . . Maybe new information technology will continue to undermine consensus . . . Or maybe the coronavirus will inspire a new sense of global solidarity. Maybe we will renew and modernize our institutions . . . Maybe international cooperation will expand."

Both of these possibilities—solidarity or division—can lead to wildly different yet plausible outcomes. But we cannot and should not simply wait for any given future to emerge. Rather, we need to enable and encourage the future we want. There are ways to build consensus, even solidarity, around specific societal goals. So let's leave a legacy for which future generations will thank us.

I repeat: global problems require global solutions, but our global institutions aren't up to the job. As with the pandemic, responsibility for addressing these problems typically falls back on the nation-state, even though contagion doesn't respect borders. However, I've often spoken about what I call the asymmetry of time and space: our biggest problems (and opportunities) are typically complex, long term, and cross-border, but our politics (and often our economics) are short term and national at best. Pandemics, climate change, desperate migration, and cybercrime are all obvious examples of just such multifaceted crises that our small-minded, short-term national politics struggle to deal with. As Jean-Claude Juncker, former president of the European Commission, would attest: "We all know what to do, but we don't know how to get re-elected once we have done it."

This is a very serious problem beyond the national level, which is why later in the book I'll advocate for a complete overhaul of our international institutions and treaty organizations—or, if necessary, the creation of new international bodies and arrangements that leapfrog over creaky old ones that can't easily be fixed or timely wound down.

For now, though, it's only at the level of nation-states, and increasingly region-states, provinces, and cities (with visionary local officials), where we can get things done. In fact, the mid-2020 update of the respected Edelman Trust Barometer, a two-decade-old annual trust and credibility survey measuring public trust around the world in business, government, the media, and NGOs, finds the coronavirus pandemic has seen government become the most trusted sector of society around the world, and—particularly in America—the rise of public trust in local and state governments.

Richard Edelman, creator of the Barometer and CEO of leading global communications firm Edelman, told me, "It stunned me that government is the most trusted institution in the world because this is a much bigger reaction than in 2001 or 2008 when we had 9/11 and the Great Recession. This is more like World War II, where it's global. It's having a serious effect on values. People are scared, and so government is seen as the information source, as the relief agency, as the one who's going to find the drugs. And that's amazing that for the first time in 20 years, Paul, that we've been following it, it's the first time government's ever been the most trusted institution."

As the Edelman Trust Barometer showed in 2020, governments that most forcefully and clearly attempted to protect public health from the ravages of COVID-19 engendered popular trust. However, governments that failed to do so consistently saw their support erode, as shown by subsequent survey results that highlighted falling trust in government as the pandemic wore on and many governments failed to control the spread. Other institutions, especially private-sector players, which have been perceived as less authentic or clear about the principles guiding their actions in response to the pandemic, also have lost public trust.

As regards another global threat—climate change—although the Trump administration showed little besides disdain for climate science, close to five hundred American mayors committed their cities to the adoption of the Paris Climate Agreement goals. The C40, a network of the world's megacities representing close to a billion citizens and a quarter of the global economy, have likewise committed to addressing climate change. This group includes some of America's largest cities, among them New York, Los Angeles, Houston, and Chicago. We should be proud that our local leaders rose to the challenge when our national government fell short. But it's long past time for the US federal government itself, until recently a no-show on climate change, to reengage with this ticking time bomb, as nearly constant climate crises show: hurricanes, wildfires, droughts, flooding, even snow and infrastructure-disabling subfreezing temperatures throughout Texas and Oklahoma. Mayors can only do so much. And so it is encouraging indeed to see Joe Biden demonstrating renewed, urgent resolve from his earliest days in office to raise the US commitment to address climate change to a new level, by following the science and using the full powers of the Federal government across all of its agencies at home, and its influence abroad beginning with rejoining the Paris Agreement. Biden's 2021 Earth Day pledge to dramatically reduce US emissions within ten years is exactly the kind of "big goal" our country needs to get back on track as a global leader on these critical issues.

If we're thinking about big goals around which to rally, you can't get much bigger than fighting climate change, since it's a very complex global problem with enormous consequences that will literally affect the very survival of the planet. That some politicians continue to question climate change's existence is beyond baffling and actively harmful. As Michael Mann, geophysicist and director of Penn State's Earth System Science Center, said on CBS: "There's about as much scientific consensus about human-caused climate change as there is about gravity." Unfortunately, the Trump administration chose denial and inaction and, as the *New York Times* reported, attempted to undermine the National Climate Assessment—a major US report written by leading experts—in an effort to keep up the charade.

Keeping with the theme of this book, we didn't need to accept that the United States was destined to remain a country that denied climate change. That's why the US federal government had to step up and lead nationally and reassert itself globally—as the Biden administration has begun to do. Rejoining the 2015 Paris Climate Agreement is only a first, if important, symbolic step. But, as President Biden has repeatedly noted and as reflected in his ambitious infrastructure plan, we also need to make a large, concerted effort to create a clean-energy national economy with net-zero emissions by 2050. We have the tools to do so, like widely available solar and wind technology, rapidly advancing electric vehicles, and a growing battery market. And the good news is that these aren't just taking off in liberal, climate-conscious parts of the country. Can you guess the state with the most wind power capacity? It's not California or New York. It's Texas. Pretty soon, Texas will also have the second-largest solar panel capacity in the country, after only California. If renewables can outshine fossil fuels in a large, conservative, oil-producing state, then I'm confident that they can compete elsewhere. And the federal government is, once again, leading the charge by respecting and extending fuel standards and environmental regulations while investing in climate-related R&D and using policy to support broader decarbonization efforts. Biden's infrastructure plan also includes a number of critical features that will prove necessary to combating climate change, including support for electric vehicles and funding to strengthen the resiliency of our country's electric grids. President Biden is clearly committed to turn the climate crisis into an opportunity, not only to mitigate the worst effects of climate change, but also to generate jobs, grow the economy, and enhance US competitiveness. I hope that he and future presidents can marshal the support needed to advance these critical propositions to help the US reach that 2050 goal.

The United States also needs to forge a concerted international effort to promote clean energy by investing in climate science research and clean technologies. I cannot stress enough the importance of global diplomacy for this effort. We should not forget that the United States, as one of the world's largest sources of foreign aid, can massively fund green projects abroad. We absolutely can and must use this power to ensure that other countries lacking the necessary green technology can decarbonize. One way to do this is by recommitting to the Green Climate Fund, which supports emerging markets in their climate efforts.

The United States should also work with China to advance climate goals, as the two countries account for almost half of global emissions. This means having some tough conversations with Chinese leadership and holding China accountable for its actions that harm the environment. It is no small task, but with the return to US leadership on global climate change I am confident we can succeed. The people of China don't wish to breathe unhealthy air, drink polluted water (if expanding droughts allow for available water at all), or endure severe weather any more than anyone else, just like the people of Houston and New Orleans do not pray for gigantic hurricanes and Californians do not wish to see wildfires burn their homes to the ground. So the politics of climate change should compel global cooperation from anyone who listens to the nearly universal warnings of the world's most knowledgeable climatologists. Thankfully, heads of state have already showed resolve to cooperate on this issue, with a broad swath of global leaders, from Pope Francis to Vladimir Putin to Xi Jinping, among others, joining President Biden for a climate summit on Earth Day 2021. Climate change deniers wouldn't think of ignoring their physician's advice about threats to their personal health and actions needed to protect it—yet when it comes to understanding and acting on the existential threat of climate change, they put their heads in the sand?

Once again, it's heartening that local and regional governments stepped up when central actors did not, and they can accomplish a great deal on the ground while helping to reset bigger agendas. But, as I've said, we still live in the age of the nation-state, and the quality and health of one's national institutions, and the principles and capabilities of those who lead them, matter immensely. Anatol Lieven, of Georgetown University's Qatar campus, writes: "The pandemic has also reminded us that it is only strong nation-states that have either the physical power or political legitimacy to demand great sacrifices from people. International institutions have at best been able to play only a coordinating and advisory role . . . The strengthening of national identities . . . is necessary for practical reform and for wider national resilience . . . Sufficiently strong senses of national common purpose will be required."

Lieven, also a fellow of the think tank New America, writes that the pandemic could encourage political leaders to craft novel solutions. Breaking free of these "ideological straitjackets" will push countries, including the United States and the United Kingdom, to face other pressing challenges like climate change, mass migration, and widening social inequality brought on by rapidly advancing technology and automation. For the Right, the lessons to be learned mirror those that President Teddy Roosevelt offered during his term: that people cannot be left to fall into economic and social misery, laissez-faire free markets cannot rule, and experts and technocrats have an important role to play in government. The Left, on the other hand, needs to realize that broad, national projects must appeal to patriotism and seek to unify groups rather than divide them along class, racial, ethnic, or religious lines. As Lieven puts it: "Every opportunity should be seized to present the economic response to the coronavirus crisis as a great bipartisan national project, intended not just to save masses of Americans from economic desperation in the short term, but to lay the basis for a new national consensus and a new national strategy that will strengthen America and American democracy in the face of future crises."

Much of the analysis around the folly of "go-it-alone-ism" that has blossomed since the pandemic has helpfully illuminated the diagnosis for what ails us today. Some have ventured into the realm of ideal solutions. Few have managed to write prescriptions to our maladies that are realistically within reach given current political reality. This book is about suggesting those changes that can help a fractured electorate and a badly polarized society rebuild confidence in their government's ability to address their legitimate concerns with practical solutions that will truly improve their quality of life. As political scientist Kathy Cramer so clearly noted in her post-2016 analysis of the politics of resentment, those voters who opted for what have proven to be destructive populist prescriptions did so in an attempt to redress their grievances: that is, being cheated out of access to *power* (i.e., input to decision-making), *money* (the proceeds of an economy working only for elites), and *respect.*

Martin Wolf, chief economics commentator of the *Financial Times,* and a long-standing thought-leader colleague whom I've relied on to help make sense of a world in flux, recently put his own stamp on the connection between citizenship, legitimacy, and a common national purpose: "In a democracy, people are not just consumers, workers, business owners, savers or investors. We are citizens. This is the tie that binds people together in a shared endeavour."

Martin goes on to say, "Successful citizens should expect to pay taxes sufficient to sustain such a society. Corporations should understand that they have obligations to the societies that make their existence possible. The institutions of politics must be susceptible to the influence of all citizens, not just that of the wealthiest. Policy should aim at creating and sustaining a vigorous middle class while ensuring a safety net for everybody . . . Human beings must act collectively as well as individually. Acting together, within a democracy, means acting and thinking as citizens. If we do not do so, democracy will fail. It is our generation's duty to ensure it does not."

In some cases, as in today's starkly polarized United States, it will take a healing "government of national unity" to improve the national mood and get things back on track, with a sense of legitimacy, national purpose, and a new narrative that a strong majority of citizens can embrace. Ezra Klein, journalist and author of the profound bestselling book *Why We're Polarized,* explains how the US once had conservative Democrats, liberal Republicans, and a common culture linking all Americans but in recent decades has plunged into the guerilla warfare of ever narrower and more vicious "tribal" and identity politics. Author and journalist Richard Kreitner describes our increasingly nasty political discourse as "civil war by other means—we sound as if we do not really want to be members of the same country." But before our leaders can break the stranglehold of political gridlock, restore a sense of common purpose, and engineer the

fundamental change needed, those who govern must demonstrate competence and experience, and—most of all—win back the *trust* of the governed.

However, as I've explained, history teaches us that, in absence of
great government leaders ready and able to tackle the problems of an era,
enlightened citizens can jumpstart the process. Think tanks today often
churn around stale policy ideas paid for by interest groups, but sometimes brilliant minds gather in various "skunk works"–type groups (free-
wheeling task forces formed outside normal organizational structures to
enhance innovation and speed to try to solve societal problems).

An interesting historical example still going strong: the nearly
300-year-old London-based Royal Society of Arts (RSA, officially the
Royal Society of Arts, Manufactures and Commerce). It started out in a
humble coffee house, and its members have ranged from Adam Smith,
Edmund Burke, and Benjamin Franklin to Stephen Hawking in our own
time. The RSA has been an unofficial if influential "national improvement agency," tirelessly hatching and trying out new ideas. For instance,
deforestation in Britain was already a problem in the 1700s, so the RSA's
fellows launched a campaign that saw the planting of some 60 million
new trees. During the grim days of the early Industrial Revolution, they
offered technological alternatives to child labor. Now, in the early 2020s,
the bright minds of the RSA are helping a fractured, Brexiting UK society rethink its assumptions about almost everything, in keeping with its
"21st-Century Enlightenment" slogan.

Ed Luce, the brilliant author and US national editor of the *Financial Times*, told me this about our moment in history: "If populism is the
product of a sort of breakdown of serious politics, of politics becoming
a branch of the entertainment industry, then the coronavirus ought to
put a dent in that. I'm hesitant to sort of declare defeat for populism too
prematurely because I think that populists are very, very good at shifting
blame, at scapegoating others. And I also think that the sort of underlying causes of populism, which is the failure of 'business as usual' in politics that preceded Trump and preceded Brexit, I think those structural
sort of problems are still there."

Perceptive commentator that he is, Ed then offered some potential solutions to address populism's underlying causes. He stressed the need for political literacy and a strong education in civics, which he hopes will help taper some of the trends that have turned politics into an endless reality show rather than the serious (and sometimes dry) business that it actually is. This won't happen overnight—in fact, he thinks it'll take quite a bit of time. But, he noted, today's vulnerable and overstretched political institutions simply won't cut it anymore.

Ed then told me that businesses will also have to adjust to this shift by prioritizing resiliency over efficiency. Simply put, the pandemic showed us that just-in-time supply chains are not always king—remember how countries were left scrambling early on for basic personal protective equipment. Ed predicts that this shift will lead to "national champions," companies given special government support in view of their critical strategic importance, and a return to some form of industrial policy in the United States, arising both from this push toward self-sufficiency and the rising challenge from China. As he told me, "The tech war, the global tech battle for mastery of artificial intelligence, is I think going to have us pull away from 'The Fortune 500 is everything and quarterly results are the measure of all' to a somewhat more holistic and politically influenced view of how we should measure our goals."

My colleagues at Kearney's applied think tank, the Global Business Policy Council, project that in the medium term, nations will begin to build greater self-sufficiency in key industries because of many of the dynamics Ed mentioned. As a result, supply chains could either reshore (come back home) or, more likely, nearshore (relocate to countries closer to home). Ed agrees:

> We're going to see some de-globalization. I still prefer to look at it as decoupling because I think China, some parts of the supply chain are going to move but they're not moving back home, they're moving to Vietnam, they're moving to Mexico, they're moving maybe even to India in some cases. That'll be true of the pharmaceutical sector as well as the medical supplies as well as

particularly in the technological sector. That doesn't necessarily mean de-globalization. I do think bifurcation and a new Cold War is a very, very strong factor here, perhaps more important than de-globalization as such.

At Kearney, we have noted for the last few years the move from global supply chains to an era of shorter, more nimble supply chains able to reliably meet consumer needs. We characterize this shift as "multi-localism."

★   ★   ★

I started this chapter with the notion that even deeply polarized societies can come together around big goals. I think FDR's famous Four Freedoms speech in 1941 still represents what we can work toward together as a country. FDR advocated for worldwide freedom of speech, freedom of worship, freedom from want, and freedom from fear. Yet today, despite America's wealth, and given how many have been struggling economically for years or even decades, many of our fellow citizens enjoy neither freedom from want nor freedom from fear. And as we face the four converging existential threats I mentioned earlier, fear and anxiety have most of us in their grip.

I've spent a lot of time talking about history in a book that's ultimately about the future. That might seem counterintuitive, but as I've explained, we can use history to get some ideas (and hope) that will guide us today. We don't need to reinvent the wheel. Today's challenges may be different from those of the past, but the fundamental truths are unchanged: people are resilient, nothing is predestined, and leaders do matter.

So now let's turn to the future. In the next chapter, I will outline four visions for the future. As you'll see, we can indeed build a better future that addresses the issues I've raised. However, without visionary leadership, a commitment to addressing existing crises, and consistent innovation, we could end up in a world even worse than today's. So let's make sure we understand where we're heading and start making the right choices today to get us there.

PART 3

A GUIDED TOUR TO THE FUTURE

Now that we know how we got here, I'm going to tell you how we can move forward to someplace better. As I mentioned, it's incredibly important to know where it is you want to go—"otherwise you won't get there." So, I'm going to outline my four possible visions of the future of America in 2030. These visions are vastly different, showing how the right mixture of two key driving forces—social inclusion and innovation—can create a dynamic and bright future for all Americans. Indeed, *All-American Comeback*, my preferred vision of the future, gets it right: the benefits of outstanding technological progress are enjoyed by everyone, not just a select few. In two other visions—*Tech Lords Rule* and *A Fair Shake*—the country manages to achieve success across one driving force but fails to advance in the other, leading to profoundly negative social and economic consequences. And *Dollar Store America* gets it all wrong. No matter your political leanings, I'm sure all of us can agree that a future marked by poverty, inequality, and turmoil is not what any of us want.

Envisioning the future is important, but then what? It's not enough to simply sit back and analyze how great things could be; we need action to get us there. So, in this third section of the book I also outline 10 propositions for America: goals that I believe are realistic and achievable and will get us on track to a future we want. After that, I reflect on how we can manage problems beyond our borders and advocate for a "Global New Deal" that works for everyone, since all of us on planet earth are in this together.

A Fair Shake

All American Comeback

Dollar Store America

Tech Lords Rule

High

Low

INCLUSION/EQUITY

Low

INNOVATION/GROWTH

High

There is one past, one present, but many possible futures. The decisions made today by leaders in government and business—and by ordinary citizens alike—will determine how that future evolves.

CHAPTER SIX

ENVISIONING THE FUTURE: FOUR ALTERNATIVE VISIONS OF AMERICA 2030

"Good fortune is what happens when
opportunity meets planning."
—THOMAS EDISON

"Plans are worthless, but planning is everything."
—DWIGHT EISENHOWER

RALPH WALDO EMERSON would greet friends
he hadn't seen for a while with the question,
"What's become clearer to you since we last met?"

I f you don't like the direction in which you think we've been heading lately, let's do something about it.

As I said at the start of this book, there is *one* past, *one* present, but *multiple* possible futures. This simple but profound insight that few consciously consider is the essence of an absolutely critical foresight tool for anyone thinking about and planning for the future, one increasing numbers of companies and governments now use: scenario planning. Crafting alternate scenarios allows us to think clearly and creatively about what kind of future is desirable, so we can choose the best one and mobilize the resources and the will necessary to enable it.

To make better decisions *in the present*, we need to imagine and develop powerful stories—our scenarios or visions—about what sort of futures we might face, ones that list the good, bad, and ugly plausible alternatives.

Doing this properly requires a disciplined process of defining, understanding, and even quantifying the key drivers of change. The future is never just an extrapolation of current trends, especially in a world of discontinuity. And you can't simply dream up science fiction–like tales of what the world might look like in, say, 2045. Stanley Kubrick's masterpiece, *2001: A Space Odyssey*, was both great filmmaking and terrific sci-fi, but its view of the year 2001 from the vantage point of 1968 was not especially prophetic. Working at the height of the Apollo Space Program, Kubrick imagined 2001 as a year when taking a space flight on Pan Am would be as normal as boarding a jet to Paris. Many Silicon Valley tycoons love science fiction and draw inspiration from it, but it's no substitute for more analytically disciplined ways of thinking about the future.

The origins of scenario planning go back to the Cold War and fears of US–Soviet nuclear Armageddon. Herman Kahn of the RAND Corporation helped US political and military planners "think the unthinkable" by devising possible scenarios of war, peace, and situations in between. The discipline developed further during the oil shock of the early 1970s, when Royal Dutch Shell gathered a very brainy team to reimagine possible scenarios for the company, the energy sector, and indeed the broader world and global business environment. During those volatile days, I was working as a rather young strategic planner at Mobil Oil Corporation, using those very techniques pioneered by my peers at Shell.

Shell's brilliant polymath, Pierre Wack, defined the objectives of scenario planning as a rigorous search for "foresight in contexts of accelerated change, greater complexity, and genuine uncertainty." Some five decades later, that definition—and that need—rings truer than ever. SRI International (the former Stanford Research Institute), where I also worked for a decade, played a key role in formalizing the technique and further applying the methodology of dynamic strategic planning to a broad swath of government and private-sector players alike. In today's chronically volatile environment, scenario planning has even more widespread application than ever in helping leaders envision alternative futures to better manage the present.

Let me make this clear: there will never be an era without "blockbuster" crises, but they won't necessarily be diseases (although many other potential contagions lurk not far behind COVID-19). Other forces will take us by surprise and disrupt our lives and societies. That's why we need to exercise our "mental muscles" to imagine the widest plausible range of future possibilities, both in terms of risks as well as opportunities.

Throughout this book I've harped on the importance of knowing history as a guide to dealing with both the present and future. Sadly, our memories are too short. Many of us have long forgotten what might be described as a trial run for aspects of our more recent global lockdown: the 2010 volcanic eruptions at Iceland's unpronounceable (to non-Icelanders) Eyjafjallajökull, which disrupted air travel far worse than 9/11 or indeed any event since the Second World War. The volcanic ash cloud grounded flights and left more than 10 million people stranded or unable to travel in the Northern Hemisphere. Things fortunately got back to normal reasonably quickly after the shock of disruption, but I think we forgot about it too soon and learned very little from the experience. Of course, while history's lessons are critical input to developing insights about the future, today we often find ourselves venturing out onto *terra incognita*. So while history surely offers a useful guide, in a world of continuous, convulsive change, it is not axiomatically prologue.

One outfit trying to get us to both remember the past and think much, much longer term is the San Francisco–based Long Now Foundation. The Long Now folks want to nudge us from a "faster/cheaper" mindset to a "slower/better" long-term one, and they've launched a whole range of initiatives that make it a cross between a think tank, a research lab, and a specialized academic center. It's best known for its symbolic signature project to build a "Clock of the Long Now," a very large mechanical clock that will keep time for 10,000 years with minimal human intervention. Jeff Bezos of Amazon fame and fortune has donated the land in Texas where it will stand and more than $40 million in seed money to design and build it. If you want a sneak peek at what's planned, you can see a small prototype now in London's Science Museum. Musician Brian Eno coined the name "Long Now" and has even written the music the clock's chimes will play.

Long Now Foundation research fellow Roman Krznaric likes to quote Jonas Salk (someone who I was honored to get to know in his later years), who invented the injectable vaccine to cure polio but never patented it or sought any financial return from it. I remember well, as a grade schooler at Brooklyn's P.S. 200 in the 1950s, queuing up in the auditorium when the "Salk vaccine" was first rolled out to us, as it was to schools around the country in a very successful mass-vaccination program that signaled the beginning of the end of that terrifying, highly contagious disease. Salk used to say, "The most important question we must ask ourselves: Are we being good ancestors?" In our age of fast and transitory everything, I admit it's no more easy to get people to think beyond themselves to future generations than to get most CEOs to think beyond their next quarterly earnings statement. To fight this tendency, Krznaric promotes what he calls "Cathedral Thinking"—starting projects that take more than one generation to complete.

Throughout my career, I, too, have consistently tried to do my part to encourage long-term thinking in the public square, not just behind the closed doors of corporate boardrooms or government cabinet offices.

In 2015, long before the pandemic or even before Trump became a viable political figure, I was the prime sponsor and co-author of "America@250"—a multiyear Kearney research initiative and call to action supported by the *Wall Street Journal* and intended to prompt US leaders to think beyond quarterly profit statements, the news cycle, and the next election, raising their sights instead to the more distant horizon. America@250 posed a simple, powerful question: What kind of a country will the United States be when it marks its 250th anniversary on July 4, 2026? The report looked at the actions leaders could take in the present to shape the best possible outcome by that milestone. We launched the

America@250 initiative as we believed that America had reached a critical crossroads, and we had serious questions about whether the country's best days were still ahead.

My America@250 colleagues and I engaged not only a broad range of CEOs, community leaders, thought leaders, and political figures in a national dialogue, but also average Americans from across the expanse of the country. The report culminated with a gala dinner at the Smithsonian National Museum of American History's Flag Hall that included thought-provoking and memorable comments from leaders representing business, government, and civil society, and concluded with inspiring remarks from then–Vice President Joe Biden.

"We can either enjoy decades of stability and growth or languish into mediocrity," the vice president said during his remarks. "I'm optimistic that we can prevail as we have time and again," he continued, because, "the American people, given a chance, can do extraordinary things. They have never, ever let their country down [. . .] it's never, ever been a good bet to bet against America, and it's not a good bet now."

Some have asked why a management consulting firm would undertake such an initiative. The answer is simple. Kearney was born in the innovation incubator that is America, specifically the rapidly changing industrial hub of Chicago in the 1920s. While Kearney is a global firm today, operating in more than 40 countries, America remains Kearney's largest market—and our most important growth market. America plays a unique role in setting the global rules for international stability and prosperity. America's success, then, is Kearney's success, and America's future is Kearney's future.

In 2015, at the outset of our America@250 initiative, we grounded ourselves in a careful study of US history, identifying lessons relevant to the challenges and opportunities of the current era. This reading of American history reinforced an ongoing bias: we believed even more strongly that America has a remarkable story to tell. The United States has persevered through challenging periods, from its birth in revolution and rejection of European imperial rule to ongoing efforts to address the original sins of slavery and segregation. As Abraham Lincoln said in considering how leaders could rise to the challenges of his time, "The dogmas of the quiet past are inadequate to the stormy present. The occasion is piled high with difficulty, and we must rise—with the occasion. As our case is new, so we must think anew and act anew."

To be sure, America has not always taken a straight path. There were times the country stumbled, and its future hung in the balance. Indeed, on the long journey from the Civil War to the Civil Rights movement, the Homestead Strike to the Great Society, on through the present moment, America has consistently worked to overcome its deficiencies and to seek the "more perfect Union" described in the Constitution. Perhaps the most eye-opening part of the America@250 initiative came from focus groups and national surveys, when we introduced the alternative visions for America to different generational cohort groups and asked them to share where they believed the US was headed. Curiously, across all generations there was this uneasy feeling that America was headed toward the most unfavorable and ominous future, even though everyone we talked with wanted the country to move toward the most favorable and felicitous future. And, most surprisingly, a majority of those in our focus groups and our national survey audience was prepared to embrace positive policy options on such controversial and polarized questions as healthcare, immigration, education, tax policy, climate change, gender and social justice questions, and economic equity—all of which were, in conventional parlance, "liberal" or at least left of center. The big "but" here is that most Americans did not have confidence in their leadership's ability to enable those positions to prevail competently and equitably. So they were prepared to revert to a less generous but understandable "protect my own turf" series of policy formulations consistent with the 2016 election outcome.

What is particularly significant from this national exercise in powerfully imagining a different future for the US is that most everyone we engaged in the exercise was prepared to suspend belief and think outside the box. Based on this work across all social divides, I am convinced that

Americans are prepared to imagine and help enable that better future if they gauge their leaders to be capable, reliable, and trustworthy.

MY FOUR ALTERNATIVE VISIONS FOR AMERICA IN 2030

To calibrate possible futures, one must first establish the principal driving forces of change. Such "drivers," identified via their relative degree of uncertainty and impact, are essential to the scenario-building process, as they provide the chassis on which narratives are built. In thinking through different possible outcomes for these drivers—both individually and then in combination—scenario planners build plausible visions of the future.

When assessing the key themes and forces of change in America explored in the preceding pages of this book, I identified the following primary drivers of change, or big keys, to the country's future prospects:

★ **equity and social inclusion** on the one hand; and, on the other,
★ **national innovation** in both the private and public sectors, driving economic performance, the quality and effectiveness of government, and technological advances.

How these drivers evolve and interact represent both a high degree of uncertainty and a high potential impact on America's future.

Regarding the first driver, will the United States take the necessary strides to become more equal and socially inclusive for all Americans? Or will trends of growing inequality, developing over several decades, continue to accelerate? What are the social, political, and economic implications for each outcome? How might the country address these challenges?

The second driver of change raises similar questions: Will public- and private-sector innovation accelerate, benefitting governance, the economy, and technology? Or might such innovations slow? Who might benefit and how? What will be the nature of such innovation, and what role might the government play in promoting it? It is through exploring these and similar questions that I developed the visions that follow.

In my view, these two phenomena—equity and innovation—will not only drive the country's future, but also greatly impact the kind of world where we and future generations will live. My time horizon for these alternative futures is roughly 10 years, with these visions ultimately extending out just beyond 2030. Putting America back on the right track, if that's what Americans and their leaders choose to work toward (as I believe they can and hope they will), will not get us to our preferred future destination overnight. But if we're not discernibly moving the country in that more positive direction within five years, I believe we'll be putting the American Dream and the position of the US in the world at grave risk, perhaps permanently.

I've already laid out a clear case in this book that inequality, including the legitimate anger and anxieties of those "left behind" economically, is the biggest single factor driving our current political and cultural tensions. That's why equity and social inclusion is one of my two critical drivers of America's future. If tackled decisively, we will move from toxic high inequality and polarization to a level of social peace and distributed prosperity that only a substantially greater equity can bring.

I have also identified innovation—in both the public and private sectors—as the other principal driver of America's fortunes. While some degree of innovation is highly likely to continue over the next decade under almost any set of conditions, the nature, extent, and ultimate impact of that innovation remain highly uncertain. Throughout US history, periods of increased government research and development have yielded outsized benefits, not only in terms of technological advances, but also in society-wide prosperity—and, more broadly, America's can-do, pragmatic, upbeat psyche. As I discussed earlier, the spin-off products and unintended discoveries brought about by the space race have profoundly changed the world and made the United States a center of global innovation. Opportunities to coordinate public- and private-sector investments in research and development remain every bit as promising today as they did in the 1960s. The chances that the federal government will successfully pursue, inspire, and incent such a course over the next decade, however, remain uncertain.

What follow are four distinct scenario narratives that capture fundamentally different, yet plausible, visions of the US over the next decade, all with substantially different potential outcomes for America and Americans. Which vision, or which variant of these visions, that emerges will make an enormous difference in the country's future prospects.

★ In *Vision 1: All-American Comeback*, the United States gets it right. Through a series of strategic investments in R&D, infrastructure, and job creation; efforts to strengthen the social safety net and public health; and cooperation between public and private sectors, the country has reasserted itself as a hub for innovation and broad-based economic prosperity. The world is encouraged by US leadership in a host of areas, from climate change to public health to international trade, while critical domestic reforms reduce inequality and heal long-standing social and racial divisions.

★ In *Vision 2: Tech Lords Rule*, the United States experiences supercharged growth—and inequality. The country doubles down on reducing regulations to support innovation and growth for its largest and most successful companies. Taxes and social programs are slashed, providing significant benefits for those already in privileged positions—and the titans of Silicon Valley in particular—while leaving the rest behind. This is a "Wild West" scenario that some find thrilling while they grow rich and powerful but that leads most Americans to live with high anxiety about making ends meet and achieving the American Dream.

★ In *Vision 3: Dollar Store America*, the United States and most of its citizens are struggling to get by. The economy fails to get back on a sustainable track after a short-lived post-COVID-19 recovery, while the government struggles to confront mounting issues in public health, social justice, job creation, infrastructure revitalization, and the environment amid increased instability and unrest at home and abroad. Despite its best efforts, the government is unable to heal a deeply divided nation, which grows ever more fragmented amid an onslaught of misinformation on television, radio, and especially online. The American Dream fades, as does the country's hope for a brighter future.

★   In *Vision 4: A Fair Shake*, the United States, led by a new generation of leaders, charts a new pathway forward. However, this journey is not without some turbulence. Following years of government dysfunction, high inequality, and racial unrest, a wave of millennial (and even select Gen Z) leaders emerge to fundamentally change the course of the government and public policy toward what one might call a Nordic- or Scandinavian-like social democratic model. Focused on improving public health, strengthening the social safety net, and providing leadership on environmental issues, the United States attempts to reset the playing field for all of its citizens. Yet this new course comes with a downside. Restrictive regulations, high taxes, and anti-trade/anti-corporate sentiments hinder economic growth and restrict investment funding for R&D to power new innovation. Cultural and generational divides deepen, generating backlash— sometimes violent—from opponents of these policies.

Each of these four visions presents a distinct but plausible picture of where America might be headed through the next decade and beyond. They are not intended to predict the future—surely no one vision will play out precisely as depicted here. Rather, this exercise is a matter of looking through the kaleidoscope of plausible future alternatives. Using these, we can better understand how to align all of the variables to realize those American possibilities that will enable a brighter future. The priorities of the Biden administration in its first 100 days—namely the American Rescue Plan and the American Jobs Plan, with its focus on infrastructure funding—reflect the contours of the future the president has envisioned, as well as the work that remains to be done. It doesn't take too much imagination to discern what very different direction we might have been headed had government leadership not changed—or might still devolve toward should a positive agenda ultimately be held hostage to continued partisan divisions and national strife.

The alternative visions reflected in the four scenarios are intended to help expand thinking about the directions in which we could be headed, in the hope of catalyzing public- and private-sector leaders, and indeed all citizens, to better anticipate, strategize, and enable the future to which we aspire. I hope that you, the reader, will also find these alternative futures useful in crystalizing your own vision for America's future and what role you can play in achieving it.

VISION 1: ALL-AMERICAN COMEBACK
(HIGH INCLUSION/EQUITY + HIGH INNOVATION/GROWTH)

In the All-American Comeback, the United States experiences a true national renewal.

As the pandemic recedes, the country is eager to make up for lost time, missed opportunities, and failed governance. Despite progress, the collective trauma brought about by the pandemic has driven home some hard truths for Americans. It has also driven popular support for establishing healthcare as the right of all Americans; a more robust health infrastructure; and strong, well-coordinated public health institutions, effectively led and supported by principled and effective governance. Popular support grows around the need to collectively address these issues—even to the point of many of America's most fortunate being willing to assume a higher tax burden in order to advance the national interest.

But reaching this new national consensus takes a bit of time and continued pain. The January 6, 2021, assault on the US Capitol made abundantly clear the extent to which populist extremists—in this case, an amalgam of far-right groups, neo-Nazis, white supremacists, QAnon fanatics, anarchists, anti-government survivalists, and others—had been strengthened and emboldened during the Trump administration. For many in the GOP, this serves as a wake-up call for the need to reclaim and restore civility and traditional conservative values, decency, and moderation. For an exhausted America, the desire to reduce tensions and "lower the volume" of divisive rhetoric becomes broadly compelling, even while extremist elements remain—and long-standing divisions in the country persist. Yet the ultimate impact of the shocking attacks on the Capitol, and subsequent incidents of populist-extremist terrorism, is to turn many Republicans back toward more center-right policy positions grounded in reality rather than conspiracy theory. The right-wing fringe remains, even if less visible, though ultimately sees its support erode over much of the decade.

The Biden administration prioritizes policies that are popular among rank and file Democrat and Republican voters—even when partisanship among Congressional leaders inside the beltway remains fierce. On the basis of this bipartisan public support, the administration moves forward with a series of programs and other government initiatives. When confronted with the stark choice of continued stagnation and government gridlock or finding common ground to drive breakthroughs that help the American people in a time of crisis, the United States chooses the latter. While many of these legislative battles are still contentious, particularly regarding healthcare and immigration reform, they result in new laws that are more robust and "built to last." On the basis of broad popular support, these laws are able to withstand election cycles and changes in government leadership.

It is in this political context that addressing inequality and restoring the middle class are a central priority for the Biden administration and its successors. The notion that "it takes all of us" to confront systemic inequality, racism, and underserved communities of all backgrounds becomes more than a rallying cry. It becomes a true movement for much of the country as people come to appreciate that addressing these endemic problems benefits all Americans. Grassroots activists meet in the middle with policymakers to deliver substantive change on issues ranging from the economy and public health to the environment and a broad social justice agenda, with deep and broad support from across all of America.

The federal government also recognizes that these 21st-century challenges require 21st-century solutions. This means increased investment in science and technology to lay the foundation for long-term growth and strategic advantage. The Biden administration focuses on R&D funding, with notable increases to DARPA and several civilian counterparts, the Department of Health and Human Services, the Department of Energy, the National Oceanic and Atmospheric Administration, and NASA. The Administration also moves to create new agencies similar to DARPA, with dedicated mandates to innovate and create new technologies in specific areas, including climate and medical research. These programs become a source of national pride and enjoy large public support, even if only episodic bipartisan Congressional support. Grants and subsidies are made available in several strategic areas, from renewable energy to biotechnology to 5G to artificial intelligence. The success of these endeavors sets a precedent that successive US administrations follow.

These investments, alongside increased public–private partnerships to share knowledge and develop best practices, generate excitement, create sustainable jobs, and spark a new wave of innovation that positions the United States to leverage and lead the Fourth Industrial Revolution. They also inspire a generation of young talent to choose public service and work for the government. Surrounded by talent, and backed by sufficient investment and a renewed sense of the value of public service, young people choose to make a positive difference for the country by embracing these jobs.

Alongside increased R&D investment, the government prioritizes restoring the country's infrastructure. After years of inaction, the Biden administration is able to garner just enough congressional support to pass a massive infrastructure spending bill. This initiative not only revitalizes America's ailing roads and bridges, but also sparks robust economic growth, putting tens of millions of Americans back to work in the aftermath of the pandemic. Not since the New Deal have so many Americans found new hope as a direct result of government intervention.

Beyond R&D and infrastructure investments, the government moves forward with initiatives to rebuild the middle class and improve social and economic cohesion. The Biden administration stresses the need to provide Americans with a fighting chance to build nest eggs and have reliable income streams. Part of this effort includes the launch of new vocational training and apprenticeship programs to fill needs in trade jobs, from electrician to plumber to wind-farm technician. In addition to launching these jobs programs, the government invests in public education. At the core of these efforts is a focus on civic education and the promotion of civic engagement through national service initiatives primarily aimed at younger citizens. These and other programs to bolster civic education help reengage the citizenry in a number of areas, starting with increased voter turnout in spite of certain efforts to suppress voting rights and access. They also help to light a prairie fire in driving big money and special interests out of the political process—to create a government authentically of and for the people.

The government also focuses on improving digital and media literacy to confront populist extremism on a national scale. Gains in this space build public trust in fact- and science-based deliberation and decision-making, ultimately helping reduce polarization. Successive administrations work with the tech giants to combat disinformation and appropriately tag and curb altered videos and other misleading content. To deepen public trust more broadly, the government brings an array of diverse interests to the table to help shape their policy decisions, including labor and environmental groups. These efforts shore up broad support for major domestic and international policy initiatives. Washington also initiates broad, multi-stakeholder dialogues around the country on the challenge posed by institutional racism in a dedicated effort to heal persistent and recently exacerbated social justice grievances.

Such reforms by the United States are not limited to domestic policy, however. The country reasserts itself as a leader on the global stage on a range of issues, and places diplomacy front and center. This process takes considerable time—following the Trump administration, distrust of the United States as a reliable partner is high. Yet over the course of the decade and across multiple administrations, much of this reputational damage is repaired. This begins with a recommitment to traditional allies and efforts to develop new ones. As the Biden administration moves to lower the temperature of international relations through diplomatic efforts and an expansion of the foreign service, new opportunities for coordination emerge. In some cases, allies coordinate R&D and innovation agendas to accelerate technological advances in areas of shared strategic interest, such as public health and climate. Another area of opportunity is in trade. The United States enters into large-scale trade agreements with strategic allies in Asia and Europe to cement economic ties—and create a geopolitical advantage. These agreements establish new international standards, developed with and embraced by business and labor, and help restore the role of the United States as a crucial player in both regions.

Yet the United States does not merely seek to revive old deals or restore its previous position in the postwar order. Instead, the country—in conjunction with allies and international partners—leads a fundamental reassessment and overhaul of existing international institutions. In some cases, this means implementing reforms, such as new rules for the World Trade Organization that strengthen protections for international property rights and liberalizing trade in services. Development banks are also reformed in ways that give emerging nations a louder voice. In other cases, entirely new organizations are formed to confront 21st-century issues, such as the environment, regulating digital infrastructure, and data privacy standards. Whether supporting or creating such groups, the United States assumes a central role in shaping this new global order and is widely regarded as an honest broker, focused on delivering pragmatic and well-reasoned solutions. The country cannot control the actions of strategic competitors and adversaries, but in shaping the rules of the road for the international operating environment, US influence cannot be understated.

Climate change rises to the top of both domestic and international priorities. A steady stream of extreme weather events continues to hammer the country: devastating drought and raging wildfires in California and the Southwest, damaging floods and hurricanes in Florida and the Southeast, and tornadoes and severe weather throughout the rest of the country, like major cold spells in the South echoing the Texas climate crisis of early 2021. These concurrent natural disasters drive broad popular understanding of the clear and present danger the climate crisis poses. In one way or another, this issue touches every American personally. After years of intense climate denial, key leaders in the Republican party shift their positions on climate in response to extreme weather events that directly impact their constituents, reinforcing the emerging domestic consensus on climate change. While some holdouts remain, just enough lawmakers shift their positions to allow real changes in climate policy to advance. Grassroots activists join forces with political leaders in promoting science-based solutions, such as offering government subsidies for wind, solar, and other renewable energy sources; making the federal fleet of vehicles carbon neutral by 2030; and establishing more ambitious fuel economy standards until fossil-fuel vehicles can be phased out. The government invests heavily in R&D to identify climate solutions, often partnering with leading research institutions (including the US National Labs) and the private sector to fund and accelerate innovation in these areas. Public-sector leaders also work with the private sector to develop best practices for designing and building a resilient infrastructure that can withstand the extreme weather battering much of the country.

These public-private collaborations and investments in R&D pay dividends in more ways than one. In addition to the new solutions and innovations they facilitate, this infusion of government investment revitalizes economic growth and attracts a new generation of talent from at home and abroad. Reforms to immigration policies ensure that the United States is able to recruit and retain top skilled workers from throughout the world. Interest in STEM (science, technology, engineering, and mathematics) education increases alongside cross-sector, public-private efforts to offer reskilling to workers of all ages in new and emerging technologies—from existing green tech to a whole range of technologies encompassed by the Fourth Industrial Revolution. A wave of new start-ups emerges, driving progress in high technology, creating jobs and economic growth, and increasing productivity. As the US workforce grows stronger, investment flows into the country.

The government and private sector also work together to innovate in the public health sphere. For most Americans, the experience of COVID-19 has driven home the need for the country's public health infrastructure to be strengthened and more effectively coordinated. With strong support from grassroots activists, the government moves incrementally during the 2020s toward a single-payer system that offers an effective safety net to all Americans. The effects of this transition are noticed almost immediately as families are no longer at risk of bankruptcy due to exorbitant medical bills. In the new system, patients also tend to seek care more regularly, allowing chronic conditions to be managed more efficiently. Innovations emerge in the medical space due to increased R&D investments. Advances in personalized medicine, brain research, and CRISPR-Cas9 biotechnology are further enabled by artificial intelligence and machine learning. The convergence of technologies within the sector and beyond create exponential gains, generating new opportunities for tech startups and large companies alike. These advances, the innovative use of new telemedicine, and major breakthroughs in chronic disease management significantly increase life expectancy. The role of government here also cannot be discounted. The Department of Health and Human Services and the agencies under its umbrella are restored to rank among the world's best.

Each of these developments—a revitalized social safety net, reskilling opportunities, booming innovation, entrepreneurship, and a unified fight against climate change—inspires a sense of purpose for Americans of all political stripes. Populist extremists, sadly, continue to strike intermittently in the years following Donald Trump's 2020 defeat but grow more isolated, are regarded as socially unacceptable, and are far fewer in number by the end of the decade. Polarization, having grown for years, finally turns a corner, replaced with a shared sense that every American, regardless of race or background, deserves the right to live a life of dignity, filled with opportunity and free from want and fear. By prioritizing diplomacy, civic education, and research, the United States delivers positive leadership for the 21st century on a bipartisan basis, enhancing global perceptions of democracy more broadly. As the next generation of US leaders rises to power, there is renewed optimism that America is capable of achieving its highest ideals while guiding the world toward a brighter, more sustainable future.

VISION 2: TECH LORDS RULE
(LOW INCLUSION/EQUITY + HIGH INNOVATION/GROWTH)

In Tech Lords Rule, the United States faces an unsustainable future, supercharged by economic growth alongside unprecedented inequality.

Although the pandemic was finally brought under control with an effective and broad vaccine rollout, resistance persisted from "anti-vaxxers" and those who regarded social distancing, wearing face masks, and contact tracing apps as inherent violations of citizens' rights and privacy.

Despite these privacy debates, there is little doubt that technology was essential in beating back the virus. From the use of artificial intelligence and machine learning to help develop a vaccine useful against variants of the virus that manifest in the population, to GPS satellites for contact tracing, the pandemic becomes a case study in effectively deploying digital technologies to overcome a transnational threat. The US government takes notice and moves to expand R&D investments and partnerships with the biggest firms in Silicon Valley. As the influence and power of these technology firms grows even greater both inside and outside the Beltway, there is little effort to regulate them. Successive administrations take the position that any regulation of these companies would slow only their capacity to innovate and grow—and such innovation is needed to compete with China in the battle for global technology supremacy. Paradoxically, this creates an environment with little competition, and startups struggle. Those that do emerge are swiftly purchased and merged into the larger giants.

Green technologies benefit from increased R&D and government funding. Much as technology was ultimately able to "solve" the coronavirus pandemic, there is growing hope that it can similarly pull the world out of its climate crisis. There are some notable gains, particularly in renewable technology and carbon capture/storage capabilities. Wind, solar, and hydropower grow more efficient and affordable. The challenge is that there are no formal regulations or subsidies to encourage and accelerate global-scale adoption of such technologies. Furthermore, oil and gas prices remain low, further disincentivizing rapid adoption of green technologies. While some large companies do commit to green technologies, often largely for public relations purposes, most are slow to do so. Overall emissions levels continue to rise, albeit more slowly, in a high-growth environment.

Bolstered by government grants and unencumbered by regulation, other innovations are also supercharged. Advances in new Fourth Industrial Revolution technologies, from artificial intelligence to 3D printing to advanced robotics, move ahead rapidly and are transformational. More jobs become automated. Self-driving trucks take over US highways, fundamentally changing an industry that had accounted for nearly 6 percent of full-time American jobs and eliminating the single largest source of independent employment across the country. Even white-collar jobs such as accounting and chemical engineering are increasingly replaced by more "cost efficient" AI. These profound changes reshape the business landscape and leave many skilled workers—seemingly overnight—without jobs or clear prospects. C-suite executives and tech leaders experience the polar opposite: efficiency gains and profits soar as corporations pursue narrow, short-term interests to maximize quarterly earnings. A wealthy minority grows fabulously richer and more powerful, while most are left far behind.

In an atmosphere of growing inequality, political polarization accelerates in an already divided country. Congress remains gridlocked for much of the decade, with neither party able to secure the majorities necessary to pass meaningful or lasting legislation. Confidence in democratic governance, already reeling under false narratives about the 2020 election, plummets further. The Biden administration finds its legislative agenda ground to a halt when conservative Democrats in the Senate caucus with Republicans on key issues, effectively returning control of the agenda, if not the Senate, to Republican hands. Following Republican gains in 2022, only business-friendly legislation that reduces regulation has much hope of passage. As a result, policy proposals to regulate online-platform content—specifically fake news stories and hate speech—fizzle as lobbyists for large social media companies argue that doing so at scale is unrealistic and cost prohibitive. Instead, the Telecommunications Act of 1996, exempting websites from legal liability for user-posted materials, broadly remains intact with few exceptions. Internet companies are thus left to "self-regulate" their content, and disinformation continues to flow freely across the web in the United States. Large portions of the population check out of political matters, as it feels impossible to distinguish "facts" from "falsehoods" in any matter of importance. These citizens increasingly regard the government as either fundamentally unwilling to or incapable of addressing their concerns or meeting their needs. They instead immerse themselves in next-generation digital entertainment, which is highly addictive, inexpensive, and tailored with AI precision to each user's taste. Others fall deeper down the rabbit hole of misinformation and conspiracy theories, resulting in persistent and sometimes deadly attacks by domestic populist extremists.

While business leaders take some steps to reduce or even eliminate funding for the politicians that encourage such attacks, these moves fall short of meaningfully curbing them. Support for populist extremists persists, both in neighborhoods throughout the United States and on Capitol Hill. The federal government moves to crack down on perpetrators of such attacks through arrests and convictions, though some extremists are transformed into folk heroes by their supporters. The Department of Justice is accused of conducting "partisan witch hunts" against "true patriots" by QAnon believers and their allies in Congress. These dynamics simply become the "new normal" for life in the United States.

Against this backdrop, social justice issues remain. Government and business leaders take some modest steps to address them by supporting underserved groups, though most regard these moves as "too little, too late." Corporate leadership in this area is often (rightly) perceived as offering mere public-relations lip service rather than sustained efforts at real change. In an environment with such extreme inequality and a lack of consensus or understanding of the roots and implications of structural racism, progress is hard to come by. Popular discontent mounts, leading many to air grievances online.

To reduce inequality, address the lack of quality jobs, and quell polarization, the US government attempts a pilot program in universal basic income, in which every American is given $1,000 a month. The results are mixed. For supporters, the money provides the necessary cushion to navigate periods of underemployment in a difficult job market for anyone other than those most technologically skilled. Yet many detractors seek a swift end to the program, being opposed in principle to such widespread free government handouts. For still others, the money is welcome but not sufficient to keep them out of poverty. Typifying the ephemeral nature of policy in a fiercely partisan environment, the UBI program is abandoned after about a year following the election of a new administration in 2024. While it may have provided support for some, it never addressed the key drivers of inequality: the lack of an adequate social safety net, the failure to address growing unemployment, the influence of big money and special interest in politics, and a tax code written for the wealthy that permanently disadvantages the average American. Groups that were disenfranchised before the program remain so afterward with this halting failure to address a more fundamental, multidimensional series of national problems.

The international operating environment has also grown more fractured and unequal. Countries that have the digital infrastructure to support Fourth Industrial Revolution technologies—namely the United States and China—are generally able to do well and bolster GDP growth, while those that lack such infrastructure fall behind. Emerging markets are hard hit by this lack of capacity, particularly as extreme weather becomes more frequent and essential natural resources, such as water, grow scarce. In some geographies, the combination of high heat and drought take a catastrophic toll on human life. Following a push from the Biden administration for the United States to reassert itself as a leader in providing aid and humanitarian assistance, such spending is slashed when congressional leadership changes hands. Opponents of these programs cite mounting US debt and argue that the country should not be wasting money abroad on countries outside the direct interests of the United States. Spending on such aid and assistance programs remains at anemic levels for much of the decade.

The Biden administration seeks to reassert US economic leadership through the formation of new multilateral trade deals. The results are slow to materialize, however, as many countries remain distrustful of the United States, fearing that Biden's successors will simply withdraw from any major trade agreement for domestic political gain. Countries are reluctant to invest extensive resources in a major agreement that risks being ephemeral. Ultimately, some strategic bilateral trade partnerships prove possible but fall short of the grand multilateral deals once envisioned. These agreements serve to bolster US GDP but fail to transform the global "rules of the road" for trade. US leadership in these areas is not what it once was.

Competition with China is fierce, particularly over technological supremacy. Both countries aggressively court top tech talent through various incentive programs, while the United States increases scholarships for top students interested in pursuing STEM careers. Beijing and Washington also seek to cement relations with countries within their respective spheres of influence in the new geopolitical "great game." Postwar international governance institutions—such as the United Nations, World Trade Organization, International Monetary Fund, and World

Bank—are deprioritized by both countries. As a result, they wither, and there is little effort to revive them or establish replacements.

It is a world in which only those with the greatest technological capacity can survive and thrive. Paradoxically, the ubiquity of Fourth Industrial Revolution technologies in the United States and China—so central to powering their rapidly growing economies—also present unique vulnerabilities. Countries and non-state actors who cannot compete with the "big two" seek to disrupt them through an endless string of cyberattacks. While many are unsuccessful, others achieve their goals on a grand scale, similar to the Russian attack on US cyber infrastructure in 2020. This fuels the sense that, despite the rapid economic and technological gains underway, a cyberattack could disrupt a nation—and the global economy—at any moment.

The overall outlook for the United States largely depends on where one sits. For executives and other senior business leaders—particularly those in Silicon Valley—profits have never been higher. Yet for most Americans, the future is far less rosy. The vast majority have limited opportunities for reliable income streams and little savings to speak of, and quality healthcare is often unaffordable. National infrastructure is still broadly in disrepair. Outside of STEM programs, schools largely remain underfunded. Civic engagement has given way to apathy as the government remains hopelessly gridlocked. Disenfranchised groups see little reason for optimism without a dramatic change, and some refer to the 2021 storming of the Capitol as a source of inspiration for subsequent action. There is something of a Wild West laissez-faire mentality both inside the United States and internationally. It is a struggle to survive, competition is fierce, and there is no safety net for the increasing number of those falling behind. This loud, fast, and out-of-control world is a thrill for a minority of fortunate Americans. Meanwhile, the rest of the country views this prosperity only from a distance, facing mounting financial pressures and growing more resentful. This path is not sustainable for these Americans, and the risk of this discontentment boiling over—through protests or increased support for extremist political prescriptions—mounts with every passing day.

VISION 3: DOLLAR STORE AMERICA
(LOW INCLUSION/EQUITY + LOW INNOVATION/GROWTH)

In Dollar Store America, the United States faces a bleak future.

After a protracted struggle to contain the coronavirus early in the decade, the United States finds itself in a fundamentally weaker position at home and abroad than just a few years prior. After a strong push toward mass vaccination in the early months of the Biden administration, these efforts stall as resistance to vaccination hardens in large segments of the US population, particularly in the South, and the country falls short of herd immunity. These dynamics create enough room for new strains of the virus to emerge and perpetuate further waves of COVID. The virus has made abundantly clear the disparities in US healthcare, with poorer groups suffering disproportionately from COVID-19 deaths and illness. The economic impact has also driven a further wedge between the "haves" and "have nots." Large numbers of those citizens who lost their jobs during the pandemic are unable to make up lost ground, while wealthy white-collar workers—especially those in the top 1 percent—are even more entrenched in their positions of power as the virus eventually recedes.

Yet perhaps even more damaging than the effects of the virus are the toxic political legacies of the Trump administration. The January 2021 attack on the US Capitol, rather than indicating a turning point for the Republican Party and the beginning of the end of Trumpism, instead signals the end of its first phase, marking the start of a new, more violent period. Republicans who voted to impeach and convict the president over the incitement to riot soon find themselves as pariahs in the party—harassed by pro-Trump factions as "traitors" wherever they go. In assessing their political futures, cynical leaders opt to go with the flow of popular Republican sentiment, whatever it may be, while increasing waves of "true believers" dedicated to outlandish conspiracies are elected in successive ballots. The QAnon caucus becomes the fastest-growing Republican faction in Congress, and more followers of the theory, however detached from reality, are elected into local, state, and federal office.

The net result of these trends is a major political party increasingly at odds with the basic precepts of democracy itself. After having lost the popular vote in all but one presidential election since 1988, GOP leaders struggle to see a path to consistent success in a well-run representative democracy. Instead, they follow the whims of their core supporters, dominated by populist extremists, and the erratic directions of ex-president Donald J. Trump, who operates as a de facto "alternate President" out of his base in Mar-a-Lago—known derisively by opponents as the capital of "MAGASTAN." Most come to believe that power needs to be seized by whatever means necessary. Racial animus and white grievance, sometimes tacit but increasingly explicit, remain a core motivator for Republicans from coast to coast. Amid increased waves of violence by MAGA-hat-wearing populist extremists, few Republican officials denounce the violence, many choose to ignore it, and others still voice sympathy for the perpetrators.

These dynamics create practical challenges for the Democratic administration throughout Joe Biden's time in office. In addition to winding down the virus and striving to rebuild a spiraling economy, the administration faces a stream of cyber disruptions resulting from the massive 2020 Russian incursions into US computer systems. Rather than assist the new President in navigating these challenges, Republican leaders instead seek to exacerbate and exploit them at every opportunity. When government computers are sabotaged, the GOP blames the incompetence of the Biden administration rather than the foreign actors responsible for breaching the government during the Trump administration. Legislative efforts to promote recovery are hamstrung and thwarted at every opportunity in Congress, particularly following GOP gains in the House and Senate in 2022. Aspirations for massive infrastructure spending, new national service programs, and major tax reforms are effectively dead on arrival.

In such a toxic environment, many come to see the situation as simply ungovernable at the federal level. Instead, state and local officials are left to fend for their individual constituencies while basic social services and healthcare costs mount. After a short-lived post-COVID-19 bounce, the national economy struggles to recover. Federal investments and R&D in a range of areas, from public health to the environment, fall short of necessary levels as a result of an obstructionist Congress. Innovation stagnates due to this lack of strategic investment and a foundering economic recovery.

As the decade wears on, key government agencies and institutions are chronically underfunded by Congress and become increasingly hollow, undergoing massive brain drain as expert civil servants move to the private sector or retire. Public health programs also suffer cuts, and the Affordable Care Act (ACA) is invalidated by a subsequent administration without a replacement. Other social safety nets, including Social Security and Medicare, break down due to a lack of funding, while deregulatory actions aimed to stimulate a failing economy reduce protections for workers and consumers alike.

After years of turmoil, suffering and frustration mount among the general public, and confidence in government is collapsing by the end of the decade. Street protests—and clashes between left and right factions—grow more commonplace. Culture war divisions remain fierce and at times violent, with confrontations between Black Lives Matter protesters, Blue Lives Matter supporters of police forces, and populist extremist groups. These battles are made more vicious by unregulated social media platforms that spread toxic misinformation and conspiracy theories, fanning the fires of political and social polarization. Sophisticated and untraceable "deepfake" videos are commonplace, making it all but impossible for ordinary citizens to differentiate fact from fiction.

This leads many to check out of politics and civic engagement entirely, viewing it all as hopelessly corrupt. Others simply grow more enraged while staying isolated within their respective information silos. The former group stops voting entirely while the latter actively campaigns for ever more extreme candidates. Community leaders in the public and private sectors struggle to navigate these challenges, though responses vary dramatically among locales. Some cities are better able to diffuse tensions, but most struggle with ongoing violence.

Suffering is further exacerbated by the steady toll of extreme weather that batters the country with increasing frequency and intensity every year. As floods, wildfires, hurricanes, extreme heat, and more severe weather besiege America, the economic and human costs grow yearly. Some affluent areas devastated by this weather are rebuilt; most others are simply abandoned, compelling citizens to relocate. The lack of a long-term government climate strategy, capable of spanning multiple administrations, leaves these challenges to budget-constrained state and local governments. Progress is scattershot at best, but severe weather conditions continue to become more frequent and consequential.

These dynamics are also reflected on the global stage. The world grows more fractured, as an "every country for itself" mindset takes hold. Efforts by the Biden administration to reassert US leadership among nations are hampered by persistent challenges at home. Traditional allies are wary that the United States could return a Trump-like figure to power and that the country cannot be trusted as it once was. Amid increasing global turmoil, the international institutions the United States had played such a vital role in creating after the Second World War—now in dire need of reinvestment and rebuilding—are left to languish. The United Nations, the World Bank, the World Trade Organization . . . countries view these institutions as relics from a bygone era and instead turn inward. To some Americans, this represents a tragic end to US leadership in the world. To others, America's retreat represents a return to a more natural world order based on narrow national self-interest more akin to 19th-century geopolitics. Regardless, appreciation and embrace of democracy falls precipitously around the world by 2030.

The state of the global economy, and that of the United States in particular, is weak. The severe disruptions caused by the coronavirus, persistent domestic unrest, frequent extreme weather events, and highly disruptive cyberattacks have left lasting scars on economic resilience. A post-COVID-19 bump to the economy proves short lived as America contends with this litany of challenges. Trade declines and value chains are shortened as countries withdraw from multilateral agreements and enact protectionist policies. What trade does take place tends to be limited to neighbors and regional partners. Jobs are scarce in the United States, forcing many to rely on the "gig economy"—one-off jobs without long-term stability or benefits. Scarce high-paying jobs go exclusively to the well connected. This tendency is also evident within the US government as corruption takes hold later in the decade. Big money and special interests are central to all major decisions and government hires. One must "pay to play" for any senior government position. At the same time, most Americans are living from paycheck to paycheck.

The quality of education in the United States also suffers, as Biden-era investments early in the decade run dry and are deprioritized in successive administrations. Public schools are woefully underfunded and many, particularly in low-income areas, are shuttered, as birth rates decline among a stressed and distressed public. Funding for vocational training is similarly slashed. Higher education, once America's crown jewel, suffers as tuition costs continue to rise, and more people question whether attaining a college degree—particularly in the liberal arts—holds any value at all. US universities become less accessible and attractive to the best and brightest from abroad, further straining the American educational system's creativity and finances. Large portions of the population, particularly those in traditionally underserved groups, fall even further behind. Many Americans teeter on the brink of bankruptcy, increasingly desperate under the weight of household and student loan debts. Despair is widespread. This fuels mental illness, further escapist addictions, and an opioid epidemic that has grown even more deadly, shattering lives, families, and communities alike.

By the end of the decade, the United States is fragmented and exhausted. Years of fierce polarization have taken a heavy toll on the confidence of the nation. America is poorer, sicker, and more divided than at any time in living memory. The country is a shell of what it once was on the international stage. Corruption across all sectors is widespread, while jobs offering a stable living wage are rare. As inequality grows ever wider, so, too, does cynicism in US "democracy." Most Americans are skeptical as to whether democracy still works or can even be restored. The American Dream has become a nightmare.

VISION 4: A FAIR SHAKE
(HIGH INCLUSION/EQUITY + LOW INNOVATION/GROWTH)

In A Fair Shake, the United States seeks to reset the playing field and build a more equitable, even if less prosperous, America—but the transition is not without growing pains.

The United States emerges from the COVID-19 pandemic bruised and battered. While the Biden administration was able to organize an effective virus response, the pandemic had already dealt a major blow to America's economy, health, psyche, and standing in the world. Persistent racial inequality and social injustice have added to the sense that the country is fractured and recovery will be difficult. Yet amid this period of malaise and discontent, fundamental shifts are occurring beneath the surface.

The January 6, 2021 attack on the US Capitol served as a reckoning for the Republican party—a "time for choosing" for party officials and supporters alike. While some double down on conspiracies and anti-truths, most ultimately use the opportunity to pivot back toward a more traditional conservative posture. The populist extremists themselves—those directly involved in the attack and others like it—face a bleak future as they are systematically arrested and prosecuted to the fullest extent possible. Under the leadership of the Biden administration, the FBI penetrates white nationalist and militia groups around the country and effectively shuts down violent plots before they happen. While some in the GOP argue that such actions are discriminatory, most seek to distance themselves from these groups and their supporters. Regardless, the short-term result is a divided Republican party—a dynamic that creates a window of opportunity for Democrats.

The failed Capitol insurrection serves as a call to action for a new generation of leaders, primarily led by millennials and growing segments of Generation Z. Frustrated and angered by what they see as the failed leadership of their parents' generation, and inspired by new young leaders, they organize on a massive scale to remake government in a way that they judge to be equitable, sustainable, and fair. This movement begins with grassroots demonstrations and community organizing to combat climate change, reduce racial inequality, curb the cost of higher education, and improve access to healthcare. As digital natives, activists are able to leverage social media and other internet platforms for positive outcomes with striking efficiency, speed, and operational scale. These efforts soon grow into something much larger when young people start running for office at the local, state, and national levels—and win.

This paradigm shift in generational power proves disruptive in several ways. Many boomers, particularly conservatives, refuse to relinquish power quietly. Yet efforts to disenfranchise voters through gerrymandering, onerous voter requirements, and outright suppression are inadequate to stem the tide of generational political change. Street protests and counterprotests between young people supporting the shifting political landscape and older "Tea Party patriots" represent a physical manifestation of these divisions and persist throughout the decade. Yet as the years roll on and the diverse coalition of young progressives continues to grow while the ranks of aging white conservatives shrink, it becomes increasingly evident that the demographic die has been cast and that such change is inevitable.

This new group of leaders is far less wealthy than previous generations and embraces a spirit of "doing more with less." Part of this is out of necessity—the COVID-19-induced recession and subsequent economic reorganization proves to be deep and lasting—but it also reflects a fundamental change in values. Saddled by student loan debt, the younger generation places a greater emphasis on free content and the sharing economy. A range of goods, including cars, furniture, computer equipment, jewelry, baby equipment such as strollers and car seats, and even homes, are rented as needed rather than purchased, helping create a more circular economy and advance climate goals. Experiences, such as travel and spending time with family and friends, are generally valued far more than accumulating goods. The new generation is less interested than their parents were in filling their apartments or small homes with "stuff." As a result, they tend to be more thrifty than previous generations and are able to build modest savings, providing much less consumer stimulus to the economy. They also place a premium on "going local"—when there is a need to purchase an item, local goods are generally preferred to imports, even if they are slightly more expensive.

Amid this shift in consumer preferences, anti-corporate sentiment grows, particularly later in the decade. Rather than advocate for public–private partnerships to enhance social programs, the new generation of leaders takes a more adversarial position. Some reforms, such as driving big money and special interests out of politics through campaign finance reform, are broadly welcomed. But other moves are viewed as undercutting economic recovery. Large multinationals, and the tech giants in particular, are targeted as being responsible for a host of societal challenges—from toxic political discourse to inequality to environmental degradation. And perhaps because they are digital natives, millennial leaders are particularly leery of the titans of Silicon Valley, viewing them as having grown too powerful and influential. The spread of disinformation on social media, which these platforms allowed to go unchecked for so long, has reached a tipping point. With support from Silicon Valley insiders, many of whom have turned against their former companies, the government moves to heavily regulate, fine, and—in some cases—break up companies that once seemed unassailable. The shockwaves are seismic, yielding serious consequences, intended and otherwise.

The first is that the sea of new tech regulations makes it harder for new companies to emerge. These new policies change frequently, making it disorienting for entrepreneurs to jumpstart their ideas. After an initial surge in economic recovery following the mass distribution of COVID-19 vaccines, new businesses struggle to find their footing in a sea of fast-moving regulatory red tape. Further, the lack of government grants or investments in R&D funding also create headwinds for new players. And while the new leadership is generally open to and accepting of international technology talent, and advances liberalized immigration policies for skilled workers, sentiment has turned against globalization more broadly. Moves by the Biden administration to promote cross-border trade in goods and services face backlash from the left, and consumers increasingly focus on local goods. These dynamics ultimately create drags on GDP growth and slow the pace of innovation in the United States for much of the decade.

Despite these challenges, the impact on the physical environment is generally positive, particularly given the pollution dividend of slower economic growth for much of the decade. Reducing carbon emissions and fighting climate change are top priorities for millennial leaders and represent one of the basic policy priorities on which the United States provides international leadership. Following the Biden administration's early move to rejoin the Paris Climate Agreement, the country proceeds to make carbon reduction targets even more aggressive. It works closely with the European Union to create new standards and best practices for carbon taxes and other climate-based initiatives. While the lack of sufficient investments slows the rate of innovation in green technology, many millennials opt for low-tech solutions to reduce their carbon footprint, such as driving and flying far less than their parents—and building on working from home trends that emerged during the COVID pandemic. This combination of changing consumer preferences, increased emissions regulations, and sluggish growth, do serve to reduce emissions by 2030.

Progress is also made in other areas—albeit slowly. The government is able to expand access to affordable healthcare for many Americans, a top priority in the post-COVID-19 world. Nevertheless, moves toward a "single payer" system are met with steep legal opposition, with some measures ultimately struck down by the conservative Supreme Court. Improvements to public education also take hold, with a specific emphasis on civic engagement and community service. New civic service programs are launched to offer young Americans opportunities to spend 12 months engaged in community service projects across the country. These projects have several benefits, both locally and nationwide. The communities themselves benefit from the work of these volunteers, which includes clean-up efforts, after-school and other youth engagement programs. The young Americans involved in these programs also benefit in a number of ways, from increased skills development and a sense of purpose, to a growing sense of national pride and a greater appreciation for where they are living and working. Some carry these sentiments into greater engagement and participation in the political process, including campaigns aimed at getting out the vote. As such efforts scale up, election turnout improves and more individuals, including those from diverse backgrounds, are encouraged to run for office or work for government.

In an effort to make quality education more affordable and widely accessible, the Department of Education undertakes a series of major initiatives. These include the launch of a commission to explore alternative ways to structure university education, including options to reduce costs, such as three-year bachelor degrees and options for fully funded two-year community college programs. These reforms prove to be both successful and broadly popular with the general public.

Funding for such health, education, and civic initiatives is made possible by major rewrites to the tax code. Tax avoidance loopholes are closed, and taxes paid by large corporations and the wealthiest Americans significantly increase. Again, these changes prove disruptive for many businesses, increasing costs and creating a drag on their profit margins. While overall GDP growth is sluggish in this environment, bolstering the social safety net and education programs creates a sense of optimism over the country's future prospects.

By 2030, the United States is charting a new course. After a short post-COVID-19 boom, growth is sluggish, and many of the power

2030: Four Alternative Visions of America

A Fair Shake

(Low innovation/growth, High inclusion)

- Affordable healthcare is expanded
- Economy slows amid increased regulations and high taxes
- New leadership prioritizes social justice issues and social safety net
- Emissions fall in high-regulation/low-growth environment

All-American Comeback

(High innovation/growth, High inclusion)

- Massive expansion of public health and social programs to rebuild the middle class
- Strategic R&D investments enable innovation-driven growth
- Expansive efforts to improve social justice
- Climate a top domestic and international priority

Dollar Store America

(Low innovation/growth, Low inclusion)

- Healthcare becomes more expensive and difficult to obtain
- Post-COVID economic recovery is derailed by a series of internal and external shocks
- Culture wars and rising extremism exacerbate social justice challenges
- Federal government fails to develop a climate strategy

Tech Lords Rule

(High innovation/growth, Low inclusion)

- Innovation-driven growth is supercharged amid deregulation friendly to big business
- Spending on public health and social safety net is slashed as inequality soars
- Superficial progress on social justice issues
- Emissions rise amid high growth/low regulations

LEVEL OF INCLUSION/EQUITY — High / Low

LEVEL OF INNOVATION/GROWTH — Low / High

brokers that defined previous decades find themselves with less influence than they had before. Yet a new generation of leaders has emerged to advance the values that they hold most dear—strong beliefs in equity and fairness, the need for an effective social safety net, acceptance of diversity, and an emphasis on protecting the environment. There are growing pains in making certain policy changes, and regulatory costs can be high. Economic challenges make expensive projects, such as massive infrastructure investment, unaffordable for the short term. But even without robust prosperity, American democracy increasingly reflects the views of the majority of its people. If you think this vision of America sounds a bit like the application of the so-called Nordic or Scandinavian model of social democracy to the United States, you'd be right.

Any of these futures is possible, and although most readers will find their ideal future in this chart, no particular outcome is assured. In some more serious version of Charles Dickens's Ghost of Christmas Yet to Come, envisioning alternative futures that *could* evolve can help motivate us to enable the version of the future we find most desirable. In the next chapter, I offer some very specific, practical solutions to address these big challenges and move us closer to our ideal vision where all Americans, and indeed all people, enjoy freedom from want and freedom from fear. Are those sufficiently critical "Big Goals" we can all rally around?

Since the founding of the Republic, the United States has reinvented itself and made course corrections to navigate a fast-changing world. It is both possible and necessary for the country to do so again to enable the future we need and restore everyone's access to the American Dream.

CHAPTER SEVEN

10 PROPOSITIONS FOR AMERICA—ENABLING THE "*NEW* NEW DEAL" WE NEED

"If the highest aim of a captain was to preserve
his ship, he would keep it in port forever."
—THOMAS AQUINAS

"Some men see things as they are, and ask why.
I dream of things that never were, and ask why not."
—ROBERT F. KENNEDY

Each of the four visions explored in the previous chapter reflects the wide range of possible futures that could materialize for the United States over the next decade. Without question, the pandemic forced a global reset upon the world, including a massive expansion in the scope, power, and ultimate size of the state. The question for Americans is whether they want this expansion to continue and in what form. Striking the right balance in answering this question has direct implications as to where we might find ourselves in the continuum of possible futures from what I regard as the best possible future (*All-American Comeback*) to its polar opposite (*Dollar Store America*) in 2030.

While pandemic-related emergency powers will ultimately be pared back, in my view a new era of bolder government and governance aimed at practically intervening to enhance the quality of life for all Americans is here to stay. This shift is a logical outcome of the tragic consequences of a government unwilling or unable to responsibly lead and protect the governed. The heroics of all those who have been on the front lines of our recent crisis trying mightily to protect the public have, finally, dispelled much of Ronald Reagan's notion that "government is the problem."

Traditional ideas of supposed fiscal responsibility have given way to various forms of "rescue" for all levels and sectors of society, with government borrowing and balance sheets not likely to shrink anytime soon. If additional government borrowing and "money printing" today creates some risk of inflation down the road, it's a risk we should take—much as the US did with war bonds during the 20th century—to address a global emergency with consequences far more tragic than inflation. History is replete with examples of positive outcomes from governments intervening during and after deep crises. Look no further than the leadership and bold initiatives of FDR, which enabled the US to escape the Great Depression, or the Obama–Biden initiatives in 2009, which provided recovery from the Great Recession that preceded their leadership. And now the Biden–Harris administration is a source of hope as it takes on the challenge to help our nation recover from the deeper straits it finds itself in.

This expansion of government is simply a fact, so let's ensure this bolder and more assertive government works for everyone. We need a new social compact, a "*New* New Deal" that enfranchises those who feel undervalued and advances the interests of those previously left behind. We need a new foundation with four parties at the table: government, business, labor, and civil society.

There is a problem, I'll admit: business and technology move at lightning speed, but government institutions (and societies in general) evolve much more slowly, and have lagged behind. Just look at technology. The speed of innovation and change in the sector has progressed so quickly that only now is our government understanding its impacts, both negative and positive. The idea that technology could be used to undermine elections, spread disinformation, or wage foreign-influence campaigns was almost unheard of among policymakers until malicious actors did just that in 2016.

In many countries, government is the least innovative sector, unable to attract and retain top talent. This lag in government institutional response in an era of swift technological advance was clear even in the early 1980s, before the advent of the Web. I can recall the time President Carter's assistant for domestic policy, Stu Eisenstadt, told his European counterparts urging consideration of controls on newly emerging technologies that, by the time government would be able to impose any control measures, savvy technologists already would have outmaneuvered them. Fast-forward to more recent and patently feeble attempts by members of Congress to hold the titans of technology accountable for effective oversight of internet content posted to subvert the free and fair functioning of our democracy. Countless congressional hearings have exposed some lawmakers' very limited understanding of how technology works and what its business model is, offering only limited hope that fair and effective regulation is forthcoming. Though the quality of inquiry from some of today's Congressional interrogators has improved, clearly the government's inadequate understanding of the complex workings of technology has been no match for those leading the FAANG companies. However, the suspension of Donald Trump's social media access in the waning days of his presidency signaled tech giants' emerging, even if slow and inconsistent, acceptance of basic norms needed to prevent the most egregious misuse of these powerful communications megaphones.

As for the notion of government being a laggard rather than a leader, cult British TV comedy *Yes, Minister* (popular on streaming services the world over) captures the flavor of many sclerotic public-sector bureaucracies. In one episode, a talented female high-flyer decides she can't take it anymore and resigns, saying, "I want a job where I don't spend endless hours circulating information that isn't relevant, about subjects that don't matter, to people who aren't interested."

Clearly, most governments (even France's, which still attracts many of the country's best and brightest to its prestigious and technocratic civil service) need to raise their game in terms of competence, innovation, effectiveness, and public trust. This is especially true of the United States. True, the federal government has several programs to attract talent, including the Presidential Management Fellows Program, scholarships for bright university students, and offers of direct loan forgiveness for government employees meeting certain criteria. But these programs barely suffice, seeing as the US private sector seems to claim the lion's share of innovative, competent new talent.

And in the UK, Boris Johnson's 10 Downing Street office briefly became the laughingstock of the media when, in early 2020, Dominic Cummings, then the Prime Minister's right-hand man, posted the following job description, in an unintentionally funny bid to draw totally fresh and original thinkers to the PM's team:

> [Seeking] Super-talented weirdos. People in No 10 talk a lot about "diversity" but they rarely mean "true cognitive diversity" . . . We need some true wild cards, artists, people who never went to university and fought their way out of an appalling hell hole . . . If you want to figure out what characters around Putin might do, or how international criminal gangs might exploit holes in our border security, you don't want more Oxbridge English graduates . . . By definition I don't really know what I'm looking for but I want people around No 10 to be on the lookout for such people. We need to figure out how to use such people better without asking them to conform to the horrors of "Human Resources" (which also obviously need a bonfire). Send a max 1 page letter plus CV to ideasfornumber10@gmail .com and put in the subject line "job/" and add after the / . . . misfit.

Admittedly, this job vacancy notice did seem to be in keeping with the sort of unusual, even eccentric, hiring approaches Churchill used during the Second World War to create special teams of very unorthodox thinkers, doers, operators, and fearless mavericks, as with the famed

SOE, Special Operations Executive—appropriately dubbed his secret "Ministry of Ungentlemanly Warfare." Brilliant oddballs have their place in many organizations, but that doesn't replace the need for high levels of competence and expertise more broadly, something that arguably has been scarce of late, especially in government.

Moisés Naím, whom I cited earlier in the book as a far-sighted polymath colleague, takes this view: "We're coming out of a period in which there was deep disdain for experts, for science, for data, for facts, for evidence-based policies. We saw it in the debate about Brexit in the UK. We saw it with President Trump's campaign. I hope that this will be one of the silver linings of this pandemic: that it's creating new opportunities for science-based and evidence-based decision-making to regain a key place in the national conversation and in policy-making."

The word "misology," meaning the distrust of reason or reasoning, was not in my lexicon until I first heard a speaker warn a group of CEOs Kearney convened back in 2016. Misology seems like a more common affliction these days than one could have imagined in this era of incredible technological advance and expansion of knowledge. The other somewhat esoteric word introduced at that table of CEOs and thought leaders was one I mentioned earlier: "kakistocracy," defined as a system of government that is run by its worst, least qualified, or most unscrupulous citizens . . . the very phenomenon Moisés observed when he told me he worried that these days, the world's problems are bigger and its leaders are smaller, incapable, or unwilling to provide principled, fact-based leadership.

US president John Adams made much the same points some two centuries ago: "Facts are stubborn things; and whatever may be our wishes, our inclinations, or the dictates of our passion, they cannot alter the state of facts and evidence." Similarly, the late senator from New York, Daniel Patrick Moynihan, noted, "You are entitled to your own opinion. But you are not entitled to your own facts." This is all the more true in today's world, where spokespeople for our leaders have had the temerity to assert the existence of "alternative facts."

So even though misology and kakistocracy are not especially new phenomena, they have more dramatically negative potential consequences in a globally connected universe led by inept or unprincipled leaders filled with opinions unmoored in fact. Perfect examples of both pathologies are to be found in Michael Lewis's book *The Fifth Risk*, which, though a nonfiction, current affairs title, might well be categorized in the horror genre. Lewis recounts the story of the shambolic transition from the Obama to the Trump administration, the "willful ignorance" of the incoming Trump team, their lack of interest in and even curiosity about how government works, and their ruthless prioritizing of short-term gains and sound bites.

Sadly, this irresponsible behavior was repeated four years later by the then departing Trump administration, jeopardizing American lives, livelihoods, and security. The only people who come out well in this all-too-true tale are the career public servants who tried their best to keep things running properly, despite being part of a hollowed-out and demoralized civil service that senior White House leadership actively undermined and discredited. And Joe Biden's new government will consistently need to help those courageous and competent civil servants, who have stood as the centurions of democracy, to build back capability and confidence in public service.

By contrast, the Biden transition team was a state-of-the-art operation led by the president's close friend (and my own friend and past colleague), former Delaware senator Ted Kaufman. Along with former Republican governor of Utah, Mark Leavitt, Kaufman essentially wrote the report on which the law governing presidential transitions was based. David Marchick, director of the Partnership for Public Service's Center for Presidential Transition, which has worked with incoming and outgoing administrations for decades, said Biden's transition "not only followed best practice, they have developed new best practices which will be studied by many future transition teams." He added during the transition that "the Biden transition team is the best-organized, the most well-resourced, and the most laser-focused transition team ever." Surely this was a good foretaste of the kind of principled, capable leadership needed to restore trust in democratic principles and governance.

In the aforementioned 1910 speech in Kansas, Teddy Roosevelt spoke of the need for a "moral awakening . . . without which no wisdom of legislation or administration really means anything." In his mind, the government needed such an awakening to help it refocus on what should always be its top priority: the welfare of the people. We need that kind of moral awakening now, perhaps on an even greater scale than what Teddy envisioned.

So, what should a more innovative government be doing—specifically, what actions grounded in practical and proven approaches to policymaking?

Now, I'm going to be both very ambitious and pragmatic: I want to advance 10 propositions where a *"New* New Deal" is both urgently needed and actually achievable to start decisively tackling the overriding problem of inequality and the plight of our despairing, aggrieved, and often physically sick fellow citizens—who have increasingly been left behind as a permanent underclass with little hope for the future. Only with a new social compact across all of society can we heal America's divides.

Those most "left behind" and chronically impoverished and under-served among us are people of color whose cries for racial justice have long been unable to overcome barriers to advancement that are frequently institutional. For this reason, the targeted policy initiatives that follow are specifically designed to help them, and indeed all Americans.

Note that it's not my intention to produce an exquisitely detailed set of prescriptions needed to realize the *All-American Comeback*. Rather, I'm highlighting themes and critical priorities that need to be defined, refined, and adopted through laws, regulations, and other executive actions. Such a dialectical give-and-take of good ideas will result in solid, broadly supported, sustainable changes in policy.

I'm also aware that progress across these critical policy areas will happen at different speeds and in different ways, and there will be inevitable setbacks, even if I believe the time is right for all of them. What's important is that we, as Americans, don't accept defeat, and instead work to reroute institutions and policies a more pessimistic people might consider permanently derailed.

10 Propositions for America

1. *Quality healthcare for all.* Much of the policy fervor around the 2020 presidential campaign, and during the pandemic more generally, focused on the growing majority view that access to quality healthcare and the protection of public health is a right—not a privilege—that *all* Americans should enjoy.

2. *Tax fairness* to raise revenue for new initiatives, and the closing of grotesque tax-avoidance loopholes. Here again, survey data shows that most Americans understand the tax code is replete with inequities favoring the rich. These need to be redressed deftly while maintaining incentives for individual initiative and entrepreneurship, which have fueled economic growth since the inception of the Republic.

3. *To bridge income and wealth gaps*, we need new programs to provide people with reliable income streams adequate to live lives of dignity, provide for their families, and build nest eggs.

4. *New National Service* options that promote skill-building, social cohesion, and community engagement.

5. *A re-enfranchised and informed citizenry*, for whom voting is not just a guaranteed right but also a sacred and binding legal obligation with fully publicly funded elections and corrupting big money eliminated from politics.

6. *Investing in world-class infrastructure and R&D.* It's time for massive, collaborative public- and private-sector investments to restore and enhance the country's infrastructure. These will enable sustained competitiveness while providing the economic stimulus critical to a robust recovery and a reinvestment in basic, innovation-enhancing R&D.

7. ***Treating immigration as a source of enhanced competitiveness and beacon of hope.*** We need a once-and-for-all solution to our interminable and societally divisive arguments over undocumented workers and their children, as well as dramatically improved policies for immigration and healing centuries of racial injustice.

8. ***Rethinking of and reinvesting in public higher education and vocational skills.*** This will require a substantial assessment and overhaul of public higher education, with a special emphasis on vocational training and apprenticeships, and a national job bank based on close public–private collaboration to develop skills that lead to gainful employment.

9. ***Accelerating development of the green economy,*** to position the US as a world leader and technological innovator in the fight against climate change.

10. ***A reinvigorated public service,*** central to running all this intelligently and successfully, that makes government service attractive and inspiring again to our best and brightest.

And, last but not least, a "bonus" proposition: one special national project of such inspirational quality and universal benefit to all Americans that it will signal our ability to dream big dreams again. I'll explain what I mean below after I unpack these audacious but achievable policy goals.

You will note that my 10 propositions focus on filling gaping holes and healing deep wounds to restore *average* Americans' faith in our system and their vested interest in its vibrancy. If there's one thing we know, it's that creative American entrepreneurs and innovators are an unstoppable and irrepressible force, and we're the better for it. However, the very stability of the Republic requires us to restore hope to those who have been left in the dust.

1. QUALITY HEALTHCARE FOR ALL

I've already noted how the "deaths of despair" and the almost unbelievable fact of falling life expectancy in the United States are simply unconscionable in the world's richest country. We see in my *Dollar Store America* vision what could happen if these dire circumstances remain unchecked and insufficiently addressed. So the first order of business has to be universal healthcare, once and for all, like every other advanced country. Access to quality healthcare must be seen as a fundamental right, period. Survey data suggests most Americans agree.

There are many different models for universal healthcare: a single-payer system in Canada, mixed public/private systems in most of Europe, and a purely private but regulated system in Switzerland. For the United States, expanding and improving the Affordable Care Act is probably the most direct path to healthcare for all US citizens, as a right. *All-American Comeback* depicts how universal healthcare would provide a safety net that ensures Americans no longer fear bankruptcy from getting sick, while improving their overall health. Sick people will be more inclined to seek treatment earlier if they are not worried about devastating costs. This results in better health outcomes and ultimately reduces costs across the system. The time has come for the United States to leave no person behind when it comes to healthcare, and we can surely find the right model to make that happen.

2. TAX FAIRNESS AND RAISING REVENUE FOR NEW INITIATIVES

To expand the ACA and fund new programs, we must ensure that corporations and wealthier people pay their fair share, something to which President Joe Biden is committed. Up to now, clever lawyers and accountants have found legal ways of dodging or reducing their liability (never mind the large scale of illegal tax evasion). Ever heard of a "Double Irish with a Dutch Sandwich"? Though it sounds like something on a pub menu, it's actually the largest tax avoidance scheme in human history. This loophole is now closed, but every manner of respectable company, including Google, has used it. Companies channeled profits through an Irish subsidiary, which then passed them through a Dutch subsidiary, and then finally to a second Irish entity headquartered in a tax haven like Bermuda. Big revenues and profits, but no tax payable!

Both *Tech Lords Rule* and *Dollar Store America* posit futures where tax policies either continue along their current path or grow even more inequitable. The result in both cases is higher costs—economic and societal—for the vast majority of Americans and ever-rising inequality. We must bar these kinds of esoteric provisions and massive tax avoidance schemes that game the system via offshore vehicles and differences in countries' tax laws. But we also must adjust the tax code to ensure rates are more uniformly progressive. And while we're revising our tax system, let's finally simplify it, so that it is no longer the world's most mind-bogglingly complex, requiring legions of skilled accountants to navigate.

3. BRIDGING INCOME AND WEALTH GAPS

Too many of today's children are born into poverty, or to parents saddled with medical or educational debt, and start life 10 spaces back on the playing board. To overcome this, some have suggested that newborn children in the United States, perhaps apart from those of well-off families, should get lifetime "opportunity accounts," funded by the government with annual grants of up to $2,000 that grow and accumulate. Then, when people turn 18, they can draw on this capital for specified purposes: higher education or vocational training, home ownership, or starting a small business.

This kind of program could also address existing racial wealth gaps. A reminder of how wide these discrepancies are: white families' average net worth is almost 10 times greater than Black families', according to the Brookings Institution. In other words, many white kids have an advantage over their Black peers simply because they happened to be born into wealthier families. In practice, this means that racial inequality persists over generations. Opportunity accounts can help level this playing field by giving children born into poorer families seed money to help fund their futures.

W. Brian Arthur, whose far-sighted ideas I mentioned earlier, believes that some form of Universal Basic Income (UBI) will probably be necessary. He points out that Milton Friedman—free-market libertarian hero and Nobel Prize winner in Economics—was actually, if surprisingly, an early advocate of some forms of UBI, describing it as a "negative income tax." Milton Friedman's free-market ideological ally and fellow Nobel laureate Friedrich von Hayek, another libertarian icon, also supported early ideas of what we now call UBI. Today UBI is typically defined as a periodic government payment to all citizens of a given country or population without a means test or work requirement.

Naturally, some have worried about the budget implications of doling out such "free money" indefinitely, along with the possible disincentives to work if the UBI payments are sufficient to live on, even if very modestly. And of course, having a respectable income from a job is more than just a paycheck. As then-candidate Joe Biden reminded Americans on many occasions, his father noted that "a job is about a lot more than a paycheck. It's about your dignity. It's about respect. It's about your place in the community." Biden would go on to say, based on his own experience as a child whose father had lost his job, that a job "is about being able to look your child in the eye and say, honey, it's going to be okay, and mean it, and know it's true."

But if Brian Arthur is right that our increasingly AI-powered "autonomous economy" will be more a creator of wealth than of large numbers of jobs, UBI may become a necessity for both social peace and to keep consumer buying power going. In fact, though he doesn't expect some utopia to come out of this, Brian does expect Americans might eventually see four-day work weeks, longer vacations, and paid volunteer roles in the community as a kind of leisure dividend of the AI age. That's what we might get when we offshore work not to China, but to artificial intelligence.

It looks like more people are agreeing with Brian, too. A 2020 Edelman Trust Barometer, released that January, found more people feared losing their jobs to the gig economy than to immigrants or outsourcing.

In *Tech Lords Rule*, we explore a situation in which the government dabbles in UBI but fails to commit long term to the program, yielding mixed results. We may not be ready for UBI just yet, but it's time to prepare options for it and continue experimenting, as a wide range of countries, from Germany to Kenya, are doing.

Amazingly to some, the oil-rich, generally conservative, Republican-leaning state of Alaska has had a form of UBI for decades. The Alaska Permanent Fund, which is the state's equivalent of a sovereign wealth fund, has been paying eligible state residents an annual dividend from investment of its accumulated public oil revenues since 1982. The yearly payment isn't nearly large enough to fit the current definition of UBI, but it has been a successful and popular program, and shows one way to finance UBI-type policies, especially in those jurisdictions with forms of accumulated public wealth or publicly owned revenue-generating assets. However, for any UBI to work effectively, it would have to be instituted nationally, much like Social Security, to help level the national playing field and ensure that polarizing regional divides can be bridged.

Such plans made it onto the Democratic 2020 presidential nomination stage even before the pandemic with candidate Andrew Yang's "Freedom Dividend" proposal to give every American adult $1,000 a month in UBI as a way to offset job losses from automation, paid for with a new 10-percent value-added tax on goods and services. One hundred sixty of the world's 193 countries have such a tax, as it's a very simple and economically efficient way to generate revenue that keeps loopholes firmly closed and makes tax evasion difficult.

Germany's UBI trial is seeking to discern if the program actually reduces income inequality. More countries will no doubt do the same. In the meantime, over a dozen US cities, including Atlanta, Los Angeles, Newark, and St. Paul, have launched "Mayors for a Guaranteed Income," a network of local leaders and municipalities who are experimenting with UBI-like programs.

The early results of basic income trials look promising. One experiment in Ontario, Canada, validated that these programs yield benefits, finding that participants used the extra cash as intended, for instance, to enroll in higher education. Other trials have shown that basic income programs can be particularly useful in getting the chronically unemployed back into the job market. In the US, cities that have experimented with basic income also note that it looks promising. Stockton, California, for instance, found that providing residents of high-poverty neighborhoods $500 per month helped recipients meet everyday needs and manage unforeseen financial stresses. Given its early success, the city decided to extend the experiment for an additional six months, and Stockton's then-mayor founded the group Mayors for a Guaranteed Income mentioned earlier. And in Finland, one trial showed that UBI recipients reported greater trust in societal institutions and other people than a control group did. Further, the experience many economies, including the United States', have had with COVID-19 payments to those left underemployed or jobless by the pandemic might pave the way for more reasoned consideration of such schemes. A better-educated and ever-expanding workforce that has faith in institutions would benefit all of us, even if some of us might need to pay a bit more in taxes to fund it. If some form of UBI gets more people into school and the job market, that sounds like an investment worth making.

These are some examples of the kind of concrete, game-changing initiatives that can address the needs of Americans otherwise left behind and alter the toxic income and wealth inequality confronting them.

You can't have stable and robust capitalism and capitalists if a substantial percentage of the population has little or no capital and is not participating in or benefitting from wealth creation—and is only becoming angrier. This is the classic zero-sum proposition. We either all benefit from getting it right, or we all lose from getting it wrong. Prominent JPMorgan Chase CEO Jamie Dimon was already saying before the pandemic that we need a new Marshall Plan for America and the world. And he's right.

Ed Luce, the *Financial Times*'s US national editor and brilliant observer of America I mentioned earlier, advocates a Marshall Plan for the middle class to help ease political polarization, noting how other countries like Denmark have invested in overhauling their education systems, training workers for their entire lives, and creating their own New Deal for the gig economy, with appropriate expansion of the social safety net to protect those displaced by technology revolutions and changes in workforce requirements. Perhaps it's programs like these that keep Denmark and its Nordic neighbors like Finland at the top of the World Happiness Rankings.

In short, we need to be open to experimentation, including with ideas that are being tried in other jurisdictions and countries, to find and implement what can work for America.

4. NEW FORMS OF NATIONAL SERVICE TO ENHANCE SKILL BUILDING AND SOCIAL COHESION

National Service used to be in demand only during times of war (think of the dreaded draft), but policymakers today are realizing its many benefits besides defense. Peaceful Scandinavia, for example, is seeing the return to conscription and National Service, and it's not just because of a militarily resurgent Russia; rather, young adults can build skills, character, and it can foster nationwide social cohesion. But that would be too much for most countries, so another interesting experiment is France's new one-month blended military and civilian National Service for young people. Switzerland, not a country in any particular national security danger, has long made military and (to a lesser degree) civilian National Service a cornerstone of its social cohesion in a very heterogeneous small country with four official languages. In the Swiss Army, every soldier starts at the bottom, as a private, whether one's parents are billionaires or shopkeepers.

Should we consider some kind of American National Service? Do today's rising generations need a reinvigorated Peace Corps, VISTA, AmeriCorps, and even newer program initiatives still to be created? In *All-American Comeback* and *A Fair Shake*, we explore the possibility of a government push for civic engagement through a combination of increased educational investment and the launch of new civil service programs aimed primarily at young Americans. While such large-scale efforts may seem hard to imagine today, they are not without precedent. These programs have historically been very popular among the nation's youth.

Let me tell you a bit about how the Peace Corps was born. When campaigning for the presidency, Senator John F. Kennedy gave an impromptu late-night speech to eager students at the University of Michigan. In his remarks, he asked the students how many would be willing to use their technical skills while serving abroad in developing countries or as part of the Foreign Service. Overwhelmed by the students' enthusiasm, he carried the idea of a new program—one that would give American youth the opportunity to undertake such work—into the Oval Office as the Peace Corps. Young Americans' enthusiasm for this work is still going strong; Peace Corps admission is highly competitive, with a low and very selective acceptance rate in line with some of the nation's elite universities.

Aside from imbuing participants with a sense of public service, these kinds of programs can also expose young people to others with backgrounds different from their own, fostering a greater sense of camaraderie and national togetherness. Some of America's most diverse institutions, both racially and socioeconomically, are government entities like the United States military. Non-Hispanic whites make up slightly over half of its ranks, while personnel of Hispanic, Black, and other racial origins make up the other half—demographics that largely track with the country as a whole. How many Fortune 500 companies or elite universities can claim to be equally diverse?

It's worth remembering that of all FDR's New Deal programs, probably the "CCC"—the Civilian Conservation Corps—was the most popular and iconic during that era. The CCC ran from 1933 to 1942 (when America needed personnel for World War II after Pearl Harbor) and enrolled unemployed young Americans aged 17 to 28. During the CCC's run, some three million young people, many penniless and even malnourished, found meaningful physical work in the great outdoors on various conservation projects, from flood and erosion control to rural road repairs. In addition to pay, room, and board, they gained physical conditioning, comradeship, self-respect, and improved morale, as well as skill building that boosted their future employment prospects. Those who participated never forgot what the CCC gave them. The program also partly anticipated the environmental initiatives of future decades. The Biden administration's intention to establish a Civilian Climate Corps might well be the modern equivalent, with thousands of committed young Americans helping to conserve public lands, enhance community resilience, and undo some of the most harmful effects of climate change.

Bloomberg editor-in-chief John Micklethwait and *Economist* political editor Adrian Wooldridge take the view that "America would gain enormously if every young man and woman was expected to work eighteen months for the government before the age of twenty-five, serving in some category or another . . . This would once again force Americans to mix across class lines and help draw a fragmented country together. If Harvard's gilded youth were forced to dig roads and guard prisons alongside school dropouts from Compton and the Bronx, they might take more interest in both the roads and the dropouts."

When I asked Dr. Jürgen Hambrecht, then-chairman of Germany's BASF (historically the world's largest chemical company) and also one of Europe's most respected business statesmen, what really launched his amazing career, this was his answer: "Paul, this may surprise you, but the first really formative experience for me was doing two years of national service. I really didn't want to burden my parents with the cost of a relatively long-lasting university education, and I wanted to be more independent. I became an officer, and this was, for me, a highly interesting experience by the way: in the military, you realize there are many different kinds of people, with different family situations, levels of talent, maturity, and challenges, but you still have to learn to motivate all of them. Very different from being a high school student!"

I've been lucky to have spent many years working with Jürgen and BASF, including, back in the early and mid-2000s, on their visionary

BASF 2015 scenario planning project, designed to prepare the company for whatever the world might throw at them or look like in 2015. (Fortunately, a lot of our decade-plus foresight, forged with a very talented BASF team, was correct, even prophetic, if you don't mind my saying so.)

5. RE-ENFRANCHISING OUR CITIZENS, WHILE PURGING BIG MONEY FROM POLITICS

Voting is not just a citizen's right; it's arguably a sacred duty. That's why it's compulsory in Australia, Singapore, and part of Switzerland, to name 3 of the 22 countries that take this interesting approach to nudging the public toward greater civic engagement. Worth studying, or even adopting? It is not a coincidence that the two visions with the least amount of social cohesion—*Tech Lords Rule* and *Dollar Store America*—are also the two in which citizens are *least* engaged with the voting process, and in which many have checked out of civic engagement entirely.

At a minimum, we must ensure universal, easy access to polling for *all* citizens. This means making voting equally easy for rich and poor, Black and white, young and old, able-bodied and disabled. Evidence from smartphone data suggests that residents of wholly Black neighborhoods spend an average of 29 percent longer waiting to vote than residents of completely white neighborhoods. With modern technology, early voting, and mail-in voting, we have many tools to improve the process and finally end discriminatory practices. And we saw how concerted and dogged voter registration and voter protection drives, as those spearheaded in Georgia by that state's former gubernatorial candidate, Stacey Abrams, made an extraordinary difference in electoral outcomes.

The visionary For the People Act, a major voting rights plan that aims to once and for all end these inequities, is an excellent example of the type of action needed, even if ultimately not enacted in its original form. We now have brewing major partisan battles over post-2020 election voting rights initiatives, with the Democratic Congress advancing comprehensive reforms intended to preempt numerous state

Republican legislative proposals to restrict voter rights and access—with the first volley having been fired by Georgia's enactment of restrictive legislation. Regrettably we appear to be locked in what will invariably be a sustained partisan battle over those fundamental democratic principles around which all Americans should rally.

If we're really serious about ensuring everyone's ability to vote, we should also make election day a federal holiday so that citizens do not have to worry about missing work or losing hourly wages while waiting to cast their ballot, which as we saw in 2020 could take almost a full day. We could also consider automatically registering all adult US citizens, relieving them of bureaucratic burdens like paperwork. Early studies show that this process seems to encourage more people to vote. And we have a great 2020 base off of which to work, with the highest projected turnout since 1908 and the largest number of Americans ever to vote in a national election.

We cannot allow the spectacle of another replay of the presidential election result controversies of 1996 and 2020. Just as the American public demanded a return to decency in governance and respect for democracy after the debacle of the Nixon administration with the election of Jimmy Carter in 1976, so, too, does the outcome of the election of 2020 provide similar evidence of support for every action necessary to ensure the US never again comes so close to anarchy. As President-elect Biden said in his acceptance speech, Americans voted for a leader committed to "marshal the forces of decency and the forces of fairness," and to restore and repair our cherished democracy. Regrettably, we had to learn the hard way that democratic practices that we assumed wouldn't need to be codified must be enshrined in law, so that we never again need rely on our leaders' goodwill, morality, and adherence to tradition.

On the positive side, the American people seem more ready and willing than ever to exercise their right to vote, with 2020 being a record-breaking year for turnout. Joe Biden won with more votes than any other presidential candidate in our nation's history, amassing over 81 million. The candidate to score the second highest number of votes is

Donald Trump, who got just over 74 million in 2020. Regardless of political leanings, we should all be celebrating the fact that more Americans than ever wanted to engage.

While we're on the topic of elections and politics, one can't avoid discussing the painful chronic failure, up to now, of campaign finance reform. When it comes to money flooding into politics, the United States really is #1 in the world, unfortunately, and many have given up hope of any meaningful change. Spending on the 2020 election reached $14 billion, a historical record and double 2016 levels. Washington is drowning in cash from "super PACs," industry lobbyists, and special interests of every description. My four visions for America reflect the implications of this money in politics for our future. In *Tech Lords Rule* and *Dollar Store America*, money in politics continues to flow freely, providing outsized advantages to special interests and big businesses, irrespective of the public good. In contrast, *All-American Comeback* and *A Fair Shake* show different approaches the country could take to confront this central challenge, with generally positive outcomes for societal cohesion. I, as a lifelong (centrist) Democrat, would be only too happy to see my own party give up all its traditional sources of big money support, if we can finally bring the era of unlimited spending to an end and fund our political process equitably and publicly.

A big hurdle lies in two well-known US Supreme Court decisions of 2010 (*Citizens United*) and 2014 (*McCutcheon*), which ruled that limits on campaign contributions are unconstitutional, as they violate the First Amendment right to free speech. You can disagree with those rulings if you like, or wish for the almost surely unattainable: a constitutional amendment that would redefine "free speech" protections in a way that curbs big money politics. Of course, quite a few Americans would also like to do away with or redefine the Electoral College, but such a constitutional amendment has been out of reach. So, 15 states and the District of Columbia have committed themselves in principle to an Electoral College workaround called the National Popular Vote Interstate Compact, which would bind their electors to vote for whomever wins the national popular vote. But the effort has stalled for lack of support from a sufficient number of additional (mostly Republican-leaning) states. Another idea to give more balance to the Electoral College and enfranchise more Americans is to admit both the District of Columbia and Puerto Rico (should it wish to proceed) as fully fledged US states.

For my part, I'd prefer to begin with achieving the possible and doable. We must pass the sort of laws many in Congress have already proposed to force so-called dark money donors to disclose their identities. Demanding transparency from organizations on their donors, including 501(c)(4)s, often referred to as "dark money" groups, would be a good first step. Congress could follow up with further action that would require groups to reveal donors behind advertisements, for instance. The Honest Ads Act, first introduced in 2017 with bipartisan support and then included in 2021 under the For the People Act, could also help by requiring large digital platforms to keep public records of political advertisements that show the ad's target audience, views generated, and the ad's purchaser. We already have such rules for television and radio ads, so there is no reason why we can't extend this to social media platforms. It is a pity that these attempts to strengthen our democracy are being pulled into partisan battles, but given that a majority of Americans have expressed support for election and campaign finance reform, I am hopeful that change can happen.

Among other practical proposals would be for the government to match small donations to help level the playing field. The House of Representatives initiative in 2019, H.R. 1, also known as the 'For the People Act' that I referenced earlier, would, among other things, have the federal government match donations up to $200 for Presidential and congressional campaigns by up to six to one. A mixture of blue and red states, and the nation's capital, already have campaign finance matching programs. (A note to my readers outside the United States: in American politics, blue means progressive, red means conservative—the exact opposite of those meanings in many other countries, and another sign of American exceptionalism.) While this Democratic bill passed in the House in 2021, it has been met with fierce partisan resistance. Ultimately there will be no way to restore trust in the integrity of our democratic process without working through these differences to find new legislative remedies that substantially reduce the power of big money in politics while standing the test of constitutionality.

6. INVESTING IN WORLD-CLASS INFRASTRUCTURE AND R&D

Our lawmakers must also focus on one of the few bipartisan issues they (theoretically) all agree on: the urgent need to improve our country's infrastructure. It is hard to imagine the US achieving an *All-American Comeback* without restoring this country's decayed and antiquated infrastructure. Previous periods of robust and sustained American economic growth developed with major infrastructure investments capitalizing on technological turning points. Completing the transcontinental railway system in 1869 facilitated trade between the East and West Coasts and spurred a flurry of further railroad construction. Goods shipped to the West Coast from Asia could be railed East, and West Coasters could enjoy European imports that often first arrived in Eastern ports. The railroad also helped bring the two coasts together, facilitating travel and communication and boosting the West's importance in national politics and business. Perhaps most importantly, it displayed to the world at large America's emergence as an industrial power, and gave Americans confidence and a sense of pride in the prowess and promise of their country.

Then, after World War II, the US Interstate Highway System leveraged the internal combustion engine to further expand the reach of commerce, industry, and the American frontier. Though plans to construct and improve interstate roads predated the war, the Federal Aid Highway Act of 1956 accelerated things by authorizing construction of 41,000 miles of highways, making it the largest public works program of the time. The result was safer and more efficient travel between states, which helped people find jobs and facilitated the economy's growth. It's no wonder that President Biden referenced this remarkable achievement when unveiling his own infrastructure plan in 2021, saying: "In America, anything is possible. Like what we did with vaccines a decade ago that laid the foundation for COVID-19 vaccines we have today. Like what we did with the Interstate Highway System that transformed the way we traveled, lived, worked, and developed . . . To this day, about a quarter of all the miles Americans drive each year are on one of those very original highways." The next time you take that road trip, perhaps you might think about how difficult it would've been before this amazing transcontinental infrastructure expansion?

If we're going to invest in infrastructure again, let's do it right. There's no point in recreating old, out-of-date services lingering into today. Instead, modern infrastructure investments will need to transcend past proposals by accounting for our larger population, climate change, and ever-advancing technology. To do this, we will need to significantly increase our R&D funding. As I outlined in my alternative visions, I believe that national innovation will be a key driver influencing our nation's future—yet America still relies on many government-funded innovations from investments made 30, 50, and even 60 years ago. This means that the innovation and creativity that helped make America an economic and political powerhouse in the 20th century—is stalling.

What's worse, other countries are catching up and even overtaking us. In 2019, China became the biggest global source of new patents, according to the UN patent agency, edging out the United States from a spot it had held for over 40 years. The United States might spend more on R&D in absolute numbers, but China is quickly catching up. Plus, China became the world's largest recipient of foreign direct investment (FDI) in 2020, with inflows reaching over $160 billion, according to a United Nations Conference on Trade and Development Report released in January 2021. FDI into China surpassed levels into the US, which were just $134 billion in 2020. Plus, countries like India saw FDI inflows increase by over 10 percent, while investment into the United States fell 49 percent year over year. What's more, our universities—still ranked among the world's best—are facing stiff competition from top-ranked foreign institutions.

Thankfully, the US is still able to recoup its long-standing FDI dominance. The 2021 FDI Confidence Index®, an annual survey of business leaders that ranks the markets most likely to attract FDI in the next three years, found that, despite a steep decline in inflows in 2020, the United States was regarded as the most attractive investment destination for future FDI flows. Despite the country's challenges, investors still want to invest here. What's more, the United States has a government that really wants to get infrastructure right. The ambitious $2.9 trillion Biden plan would not only address issues with our roads and bridges, but also invest in schools, broadband access, and power lines to make it a truly comprehensive investment in a future benefiting all Americans.

Let's use that will to revitalize domestic innovation with a big reinvestment in American R&D, which the Biden infrastructure plan is already calling for, as it would mark the largest ever increase in nondefense R&D. We can start by reinvesting in the Department of Energy's National Labs, which are located throughout the country and lately have been considered for funding cuts. We can thank these labs for removing arsenic from water, installing the continent's first web server, confirming the Big Bang Theory, creating an environmentally friendly alloy to cool refrigerators, and inventing a sponge that can clean up oil spills, just to name a few of their many life-enhancing innovations. These labs helped establish the United States as a leading center of innovation and scientific discovery, and yet proposals to cut their funding persist. Supporting such groundbreaking work should top every US policymaker's agenda.

And there is no reason our country cannot improve its infrastructure once again, as it has done before in times of need. In the aftermath of the pandemic, investing in public infrastructure is a smart way to kick-start our economy while building something that benefits us all, emphatically including future generations. What better way to support American workers, businesses, and citizens than by investing in local communities and our manufacturing capacity? Smart policy will focus on making this infrastructure climate resilient, since we know that extreme weather events and rising temperatures are here to stay. Again, the Biden plan is already anticipating this by investing in electric vehicle expansion and updating grids to adapt to climate change. In the US alone, our National Oceanographic and Atmospheric Administration (NOAA) reported that 2020 featured a record number of billion-dollar weather disasters: from unusually destructive landfalling tropical systems, to multiple tornado outbreaks, to the most active drought-induced wildfire year on record. Moreover, the five warmest years on record in the US have occurred in the last decade, including last year, which was the fifth warmest on record and the second hottest year on record globally. And, of course, millions of Texans struggled to recover from the harsh weather crisis of early 2021, which highlighted how extreme weather is adversely impacting aging infrastructure.

Rolling blackouts in Texas, Oklahoma, Mississippi, and several other states; one-third of US oil production halted; drinking-water systems knocked offline; road networks paralyzed; and vaccination efforts across the country disrupted . . . all of these adverse consequences of severe weather bring with them tremendous direct and even greater knock-on economic costs, not to mention the tragic cost severe weather exacts on human life and livelihood. It won't be easy, but if we could radically expand our infrastructure after the Civil War and the Second World War, we should feel confident we can do it again today.

7. TREATING IMMIGRATION AS A SOURCE OF ENHANCED COMPETITIVENESS AND A BEACON OF HOPE

An equally inflamed and emotive perennial issue as voter enfranchisement, and one as challenging as infrastructure, is that of undocumented workers and unauthorized immigration. It's a problem facing Europe, too, as millions of desperate migrants from the Middle East and Africa seek ways to get to Germany, Sweden, and other rich countries. Most European countries have historically had a tougher time assimilating newcomers than we have, as they are not nations built on immigration in the way the United States, Canada, and Australia are. But in both the US and EU, the backlash against immigration has been the tinder for populist flames, even if Donald Trump's promised US–Mexico border wall missed its mark, not to mention its source of funding. Even after Trump was defeated and Joe Biden assumed the presidency during a global pandemic that had shut down economies, closed schools, and taken millions of lives, immigration was still a hot-button issue that consumed considerable time, attention, and resources. There's also a nasty, even if often unspoken, racial undertone to all this. And ever since the first immigrants landed on US shores, Native Americans, the only group in our country *not* composed of immigrants, have experienced significant racism spanning the entire history of our country.

So xenophobia and racism long predate Donald Trump, to be sure. Almost every major ethnic group experienced significant prejudice when first arriving in America, from the Irish to East Asians to Jewish migrants from Europe to my own Italian ancestors. What governments have failed to appreciate sufficiently through today is that immigration is overwhelmingly positive for a country.

America has been a beacon to immigrants since its early settlers landed on Plymouth Rock, and each successive wave of immigrants has continued to build this country with their own unique contribution to its greatness. Immigrants pioneered modern inventions that we take for granted today. Since 1901, 35 percent of US Nobel Prize winners in physics, chemistry, and medicine have been immigrants. These include Dr. Gerty Cori, the first woman to ever win a Nobel Prize in physiology or medicine, back in 1947. Born and educated in Prague, Dr. Cori's work focused on carbohydrate metabolism. Another record setter was the Chinese American physicist Tsung-Dao Lee, who became the second-youngest scientist to win a Nobel Prize when he was awarded one in 1957 while at Columbia University. One of the 2019 chemistry winners is British American M. Stanley Whittingham, who was recognized for his work on lithium-ion batteries, a technology vital to the rise in electric-vehicle use. Beyond the Nobel winners, a 2017 study from the Center for American

Entrepreneurship found that 43 percent of Fortune 500 companies were founded or co-founded by an immigrant or a first-generation American. Tech companies today rely on highly skilled H1-B visa holders to power our country's most globally competitive industry; a 2015 study found that immigrants made up over half of workers in Silicon Valley. Plus, many Americans, from numerous presidents to, more modestly, myself and many of my colleagues, would not be here today had America resorted to restrictive immigration. In *All-American Comeback*, the United States recognizes the potential of immigrants, as well as the economic and societal advantages they bring to the country. There is no good reason why such an outcome should be out of reach for a country that remains a beacon of hope to so many around the world.

Immigrant groups have also contributed greatly to popular American culture over the years, from our food to our music to our literature. Who could imagine America without pizza, tacos, Halloween, and annual Chinese New Year celebrations? Immigrants have also proven time and again that they bring net benefits to an economy. Back in the day, immigrants built railroads, worked in factories and mines as the country was industrializing, and performed tasks that many native-born Americans refused to do. The situation is similar today. Modern employers—for example, in California's vast agricultural sector, or hotel and restaurant owners—have long depended on undocumented labor to do the dirty, backbreaking jobs US citizens are rarely willing to do for minimal pay. We need to ensure that immigrants have a clear and fair path to citizenship and that they are not exploited on their way to that goal. Yet these issues have caused a poisonous rift in America, diminishing our competitiveness and demeaning the country's founding principles. We need to tackle them decisively. And I believe it can be done.

Let me tell you a story: I remember striding up to a podium in 1998 at the Ritz-Carlton in Palm Beach, taking a deep breath, and then introducing the future president of Mexico. I think most of the audience thought I was kidding. The unknown man who started to speak in heavily accented but fluent English was a tall, cowboy-boot-wearing former CEO of Coca-Cola Mexico, Vicente Fox, who had been elected governor of a somewhat unknown (at least to most of us north of the border) Mexican state, Guanajuato—known for, if anything, its beautiful colonial city San Miguel de Allende, a favorite of discerning travelers the world over. Vicente was so pleased by my introduction that he told the audience that I and my CEO clients would be his honored guests at the Mexican White House, Los Pinos, if he ever became president. He was indeed elected president, and he kept his promise, which made for an amazing half-day as his guest in Mexico City that I'll never forget.

Fast-forward to February 2001, and presidents Vicente Fox and George W. Bush, both ranchers, met at Vicente's ranch in Monterrey, Mexico. To give Bush credit, he was as keen as his Mexican counterpart to solve the two countries' frictions over immigration and the border, and on the table was a new legal guest-worker program concept, along with ideas to create a path to legal residence and maybe even American citizenship one day, for those Mexicans already in the country. But then a little over six months later, 9/11 happened, and those proposals went on the back burner.

Now, twenty years later, little else has been done, and surely the problems and acrimony are more acute, especially since many current migrants into the US are often crossing Mexico from other Central American countries, complicating negotiations with more stakeholders. As with campaign finance reform, Congress and the president must finally enact workable legislation that acceptably solves one of our longest-running and divisive problems. We've come close before with bipartisan approaches. It can and must be done.

8. RETHINKING AND REINVESTING IN PUBLIC HIGHER EDUCATION AND VOCATIONAL SKILLS

In our time of career fluidity, entire job categories vanish in the blink of an eye, while new ones only gradually emerge. Both the body politic and the corporate world need to rethink colleges, universities, apprenticeships, and vocational education, not least because a mismatch seems to be growing between the skills our graduates have and those employers demand.

In the US, people quip that there's a college track and a Big Mac track, and there's more than a little truth in that. Germany and Switzerland have had amazing (and prestigious) apprenticeship-based vocational education systems for over a century. Those two countries have long put such vocational training and credentialing at the very core of their national economies and societies, so it's a model that, admittedly, isn't easy to replicate.

To date, in the US, there has been some recent success with bottom-up initiatives like coding boot camps and other vocational "micro-credentials." These can provide fast, relatively inexpensive training, largely or partially online, and offer a path to quick employability for both young adults and mid- or late-career people needing new, mostly technology-related, marketable skills. Two caveats are that such programs, a mix of not-for-profit and for-profit initiatives, provide skills with a very short half-life given their subject focus; and that this fast-moving and largely unregulated educational segment has both serious and shady purveyors. But now even Google has jumped into the game with its new Google Career Certificates, with curricula designed and taught by Google employees in such high-paying, high-growth career fields as data analytics and UX (user experience) design.

There is no doubt a pressing need to reskill our workforce, and thankfully many options are at our disposal. Perhaps we could look across the pond at the United Kingdom's national retraining program, launched in 2019, which reskills adults in need of work. The UK government is also partnering with leading banks such as Barclays to support programs aimed at young people, and in 2020, the government expanded existing programs by offering adults without certain qualifications a free college level course to help them gain in-demand skills in fields such as healthcare, engineering, and conservation.

The Republic of Ireland has also had success in using public–private partnerships to stimulate growth and provide its people well-paid work.

Back in 1949, this recently independent republic was grappling with a number of challenges, including widespread abject poverty and brain drain from centuries of emigration driven by lack of opportunity and even famine. Instead of accepting that its fate was to be a small impoverished island whose many citizens were forced to use their talents elsewhere, the Irish created an Industrial Development Authority (IDA) to support export-driven businesses. Over the years, as the economy opened up and welcomed foreign direct investment, the IDA grew more active. Due largely to the IDA and a new program of free secondary school education launched in the 1960s, Ireland went from being a poor rural country with a hard history to one of the world's most vibrant industrial and service economies. Even today, the IDA continues to provide funding and grants to overseas companies considering direct investment. Ireland is now not only one of the world's wealthiest countries based on GNI per capita, but also hosts numerous advanced, globally competitive industries. For instance, the part of Dublin that has attracted major investments as host to the European headquarters of tech giants such as Apple, Google, and Twitter is referred to as "Silicon Docks" (even if not without some domestic pushback because of the impact of gentrification and local displacement borne of a rising cost of living). Pharmaceuticals are also well-represented, as Pfizer and Bristol Myers Squibb have large facilities in Ireland. Not bad for a country with about half the population of New York City.

There's no reason the United States could not consider similar programs here, especially in fields where the needs are the greatest. The implications are made clear in in my four visions, particularly the contrast between *All-American Comeback*, in which such reskilling efforts and public–private partnerships are prioritized and properly implemented, and *Tech Lords Rule*, in which such programs are not realized, despite a desperate need for them in an environment of rapid worker displacement from automation. My colleagues at the Center for Strategic and International Studies suggest a number of remedies including retraining workers disadvantaged by free trade, linking unemployment assistance with re-education efforts, and even creating "education savings accounts," where each individual puts away some of their own paycheck that they can tap later for retraining and lifelong learning. These would function like health savings accounts, allowing people to take charge of their own education. Similarly, the World Economic Forum's Reskilling Revolution Platform brings together public and private sectors to advance global upskilling efforts, focusing especially on digital skills and training workers in Fourth Industrial Revolution technologies.

At the very least, we need to make higher education less expensive and better suited to the jobs of the future. In the 1990s, Stanford University president Gerhard Casper boldly suggested that we cut out the fluff and unnecessary expense by allowing institutions to offer a three-year bachelor's degree. That idea, especially combined with the need for lifelong learning and retraining, makes more sense than ever, if US universities might consider it. Of course others might prefer to stick with their traditional four-year curriculum—the United States can and should accommodate many approaches to learning and education without imposing a one-size-fits-all approach.

At a bare minimum, much as President Biden and our community college educator, First Lady Jill Biden, have advocated, we need to make two-year community colleges tuition free, as they continue to be a key escalator of social mobility for the bottom half of society. I touch on this idea in *A Fair Shake*, in which a younger generation of leaders, saddled with student loan debt, prioritizes ways to make post-secondary education more affordable. Numerous community college graduates have gone on to achieve remarkable things, to the benefit of the country as a whole. The first American woman to pilot and command a space shuttle, Eileen Collins, got an associate's degree before heading on to a bachelor's, a master's, and eventually, NASA. The first Hispanic woman ever elected to Congress, Ileana Ros-Lehtinen, who served for a total of 30 years, got her academic start with an associate's degree from Miami Dade College. And author Amy Tan, whose novel *The Joy Luck Club* is now read in many high school English classes, also attended community college before getting her bachelor's degree due to the high cost of attending a traditional four-year institution.

We need to relearn just how extraordinary the return on investment in affordable public higher education can be, and there's almost no better example than the institution long known as "the poor man's Harvard": CCNY, or the City College of New York. Founded in 1847 with seed money from some truly forward-looking business leaders, it became America's first free public institution of higher education, designed to give working-class and immigrant families a shot at bettering themselves. It certainly exceeded the wildest dreams of its founders, with 10 graduates earning Nobel Prizes and a roll call of former students who went on to do exceptional things in every field imaginable: the names Bernard Baruch, Felix Frankfurter, Henry Kissinger, Stanley Kubrick, Ralph Lauren, Audre Lorde, Daniel Patrick Moynihan, Colin Powell, Adrienne Rich, and Jonas Salk barely scratch the surface.

In terms of making education affordable, we should go even further and provide students from families earning under $125,000 annually free tuition at public universities, too, while increasing the value of Pell Grants, a popular longtime program to help students from lower-income families. Many of these public colleges are already among the best in the nation, and with even more talent from a wider pool of students, they (and our country) will only grow smarter and stronger.

Some may remember the visionary 1960 California Master Plan for Higher Education, which created an integrated system of community colleges and California State colleges and universities, with the top-tier, research-intensive University of California at its apex. California's once-visionary strategy cranked up a roaring engine of economic growth, technological innovation, and social mobility, and made the Golden State the envy of the world. So why can't we think as boldly today as previous generations once did?

Unfortunately, over the years, a fractious, budget-strained California has allowed its Master Plan to atrophy and fade into the sunset. The University of California remains the greatest public university on the planet, but its flagship UCLA and Berkeley campuses are no longer fully state funded, relying instead on multibillion-dollar private fundraising campaigns as well as tuition hikes to maintain their excellence. And other exceptional public universities, like those of Michigan and Virginia, now charge in-state tuition and fees upward of $15,000—far cheaper than the $50,000-plus of their private competitors, but still well above fees just 10 years ago. This all puts college out of reach for more and more hardworking families. We seem to have forgotten that world-class public education isn't a cost but an investment in future growth, innovation, and broad-based prosperity.

The late, great Daniel Patrick Moynihan once said that it's simple to build a great and flourishing city: "First create a university, and then wait 200 years." It's still a good quip, and it underscores how quality educational institutions can be drivers of regional success. For example, those US cities in the Midwest and East enjoying revivals rather than Rust Belt agonies are those that have made brainpower institutions a top priority. A perfect example is Pittsburgh, once jeopardized by the decline of the steel and other traditional "smokestack" industries. Today people call it "Roboburgh," with Carnegie Mellon University its key academic hub, and with a local boom in robotics, AI, self-driving vehicles, and biomedical research. Zoom announced plans to open a research center in Pittsburgh in 2020 and began hiring local talent that same year. It's a virtuous circle of bright young people who come and often stay, cycles of big research funding, an entrepreneurial startup culture, the ongoing commercialization of new intellectual property, and good new jobs in advanced manufacturing for those with blue-collar backgrounds. Andrew Carnegie would be proud.

Baltimore, Cleveland, Denver, and Detroit are slowly following in Pittsburgh's footsteps as millennials flock to these cities for lower living costs and both tech companies and startups establish offices there. Like Pittsburgh, the universities in these cities—such as Johns Hopkins, Case Western Reserve, or the University of Michigan—serve as natural hubs of innovation and talent. Investing in education means investing in communities and cities.

9. INNOVATING TOWARD A GREEN ECONOMY AND FIGHTING CLIMATE CHANGE

Speaking of innovation, as I mentioned earlier, the United States has in recent years been a shameful no-show in the fight against climate change, as Americans choke on thick, apocalyptic wildfire smoke and watch their homes burn or be destroyed by other forms of extreme weather. We're a nation of innovators, and it's high time we put our brain power and ingenuity to work on solutions to decarbonize our economy and become a leader among nations again.

In chapter five, I outlined the most essential steps the United States needs to take on climate. CNN personality and *Washington Post* columnist Fareed Zakaria reminds us that the Dust Bowl of the 1930s remains the greatest ecological disaster in US history, with the desperate Okies and other migrants immortalized by John Steinbeck's *The Grapes of Wrath* as "America's first climate refugees." If FDR could take decisive action almost a century ago, surely we can do even better with our far more advanced technologies. Zakaria points out that the Roosevelt administration "produced a short movie to explain it to the country . . . Government agencies taught farmers how to prevent soil erosion . . . established the Soil Conservation Service, and placed 140 million acres of federal grasslands under protection. In the last three-quarters of a century, there has been no second Dust Bowl, despite extreme weather." Biden's ambitious green economy initiatives, aimed at both mitigating climate change and enhancing US economic competitiveness, extend FDR's legacy of conservation into our own century and beyond.

10. REINVIGORATING OUR PUBLIC SERVICE AND ATTRACTING THE BEST AND BRIGHTEST TO GOVERNMENT

President Kennedy's most famous inaugural quote, "Ask not what your country can do for you—ask what you can do for your country," is as salient an admonition today as it was in 1961. If the policies I've outlined here are to be adopted and effectively executed, we need to make government service attractive again for our best and brightest, including young people, most of whom in recent decades would never have considered a public service career. Although high elective or appointive office in America is still prestigious, the appeal of working for the government has diminished, almost as though the civil service has been relegated to those who can't get higher-paying, career-enhancing private-sector jobs.

Unlike most advanced countries, the United States doesn't have a "fast-track" national or federal public service recruitment and career management process to attract and retain top talent, nor are the salaries competitive with business and the professions. Though we have some programs like the aforementioned Presidential Management Fellows Program, they are primarily geared toward well-educated individuals already interested in public service, even though the pay is still significantly below what most private companies offer. And though we have programs, like the Public Loan Forgiveness Program, to help government employees reduce their student loan debt, they are in serious need of a revamp, as Biden pointed out while campaigning for president. For many students, especially those graduating with loans, a well-paid job is the difference between financial security and financial catastrophe. Government work thus may not be a good fit for young people with financial constraints. This must change.

The founder of modern Singapore, Lee Kuan Yew, once said this, rather bluntly, about government jobs: "If you pay peanuts, you get monkeys." Singapore's government not only pays its people extremely well, but it also provides opportunities to gain graduate degrees in the UK and US, and many other opportunities for professional development—not to mention the chance to make a difference, to have a social impact in ways to which their corporate peers likely could not aspire. No wonder the cream of the crop joins the civil service there, or why the "Intelligent Island" is so well run.

Elected leaders and administrations come and go, so it's essential we have highly talented people who are excited about making long-term careers in our public service. In *All-American Comeback*, moves to increase salaries and invest appropriately in key government agencies, from the State Department to the Department of Health and Human Services, inspire young talent to take government jobs—and remain in them. This lays the foundation for the positive outcomes depicted in this vision for the future. Matching corporate compensation isn't possible or even necessary, but we can make the total value proposition much more enticing, even as we appeal to the idealism of talented young and mid-career Americans. Today, only a few specialized programs, including those of the US Foreign Service, CIA, and Armed Services (through their service academies, including West Point and Annapolis), provide such an intake and training process, along with a coherent and compelling long-term career opportunity. A reinvigorated public service can also be a key ladder of social mobility for bright graduates who have received Pell Grants—that is, those of exceptional financial need, and often the first in their families to pursue higher education.

PROPOSITION 11 OF 10

Following on my 10 Propositions for America, my bonus proposition for America may seem excessive, or even frivolous to some, given how ambitious the 10 more "practical" programs already are. I am proposing at least one additional, special national project of such inspirational quality that it will signal to Americans that we can dream big dreams again and take great pride in our country once more. Perhaps our 250th anniversary as a nation, July 4, 2026, might just be the moment to lift the curtain and launch it.

If you're old enough to remember it (I am), President Kennedy's 1962 promise to put a man on the moon before the end of that decade captured the imagination of multiple generations, the country, and the world. Perhaps Jack Kennedy and NASA weren't entirely sure they could deliver. Debates over whether the Space Program was worth the money will forever rumble on, but nobody doubts that it was a monumental challenge that called us to strive for American greatness (the real deal, as opposed to "MAGA" sloganeering).

I have some thoughts for what we might do (*not* another Space Program), but my 11th proposition is that we leave its exact nature to a competition of ideas engaging the widest possible group of interested citizens. We might even structure it as an incentive prize, underwritten by philanthropy, with the winners being those with the best and more inspiring proposals. Given the billions contemporary philanthropists have committed to good causes, perhaps some of them might even help fund the national project itself.

As with my other propositions, I think we should feel free to look at what other countries have done or are doing. Ben Franklin is supposed to have said, "Every man has two countries—his own and France." I'll admit that sentiment no longer has quite the resonance it once had, given the recalibration of the world order, changes in culture, and the shift from French to English as the globe's lingua franca. Still, the country—our oldest ally—offers some interesting examples. General and later President Charles de Gaulle, who kept the dream of a free France alive during its humiliating Nazi occupation, always said, "France cannot be France without greatness." French leaders up to the present, of every political stripe, have tended to agree strongly. In that very spirit, President François Mitterrand launched a massive (if expensive) revitalization of Paris that included the building of eight new *modern* monumental buildings during the period 1981–98. These *Grands Projets* showed that the French could still match their predecessors in creativity and further beautify an already glittering capital. One of the projects was the Louvre Pyramid, designed by I. M. Pei, which has become a modern symbol of Paris. It was a very French undertaking—probably something we wouldn't do, but it has a kind of aspirational, iconic *je ne sais quoi* character to it worth emulating.

Whatever national project we choose to pursue should signify that America is back, in every best sense, a beacon to the world and a land where no one is left behind. And, most of all, that it's an America that Americans can justifiably be proud of.

CHAPTER EIGHT

It's an increasingly dangerous world out there, as America seeks to navigate the rise of a militarily aggressive Chinese economic superpower, a trouble-making and still heavily armed Russia, a rising and important India, and too many potential flashpoints around the world to count. From military and intelligence operations to malicious hacking and attempts to sway elections, cyber in all its growing sophistication has come out of the shadows to enable threatening state and non-state actors.

KEEPING THE PEACE: UNCLE SAM ENGAGES THE DRAGON, THE BEAR, AND THE TIGER

"Considering the extraordinary character of the times
in which we live, our attention should unremittingly
be fixed on the safety of our country."
—THOMAS JEFFERSON,
IN HIS FINAL MESSAGE TO CONGRESS

In 1983, *The Economist* magazine celebrated its 150th anniversary by asking 20 luminaries to predict what the longer-term future has in store for us. Their prognostications, from an era well before the smartphone or even wide access to the internet, make for interesting reading. Here are some of their forecasts: 1) The United States will become even more politically correct, litigious, and regulation-mad; 2) Race and religion will become more, not less, important; 3) Capitalism could sow the seeds of its own demise or at least disasters; 4) Warfare has a future.

You have to admit that was a prophetic set of predictions, including, unfortunately, the fact that constant wars of various scales, not world peace, have characterized our early 21st century. Today, the world is armed to the teeth (and becoming ever more so), with potential flashpoints from Asia and the Middle East to the Arctic. History tells us that many wars aren't "planned" but emerge from accidental or unforeseen situations that escalate into armed conflict.

One of the many danger zones is the Korean Peninsula, given the immense difficulties involved in trying to engage what is probably the world's strangest state, North Korea—a kind of totalitarian, communist, hereditary absolute monarchy. The DPRK has even tried a bit of weird soft power with its "Korean Friendship Association," a state-sponsored love-in for fans of the regime with branches in more than 30 countries. Members can join special VIP group tours to this bellicose hermit kingdom, and are issued funny-looking membership cards. But there's nothing funny about the risks North Korea poses.

Unfortunately for us, North Korea is not the only country we need to worry about. Iran has shown a willingness to flout international rules, support terrorist groups, and escalate tensions with its neighbors and the United States. These tendencies have brought the world to the brink of war multiple times—do you remember in just January 2020, when the world was convinced that the United States and Iran would go to war after the US assassinated Qasem Soleimani? Thankfully, we avoided war then, but we should be doing more to ensure we never edge that close again. Rejoining the Iran nuclear deal would be a good start, even if we need to renegotiate its terms and work indirectly through our partners to improve it.

The list of danger zones doesn't stop with Iran and North Korea. Tensions along the India–China border in the Himalayas reached a boiling point in 2020 as skirmishes broke out for the first time in years. This open wound could easily dent relations between the two most populous countries in the world, with repercussions for the rest of the globe. Also in 2020, massive protests erupted in Belarus of all places as residents, fed up with Europe's last dictator, finally said "Enough." The movement echoes similar uprisings in other former Soviet states, like Georgia, Armenia, and the Ukraine, as outdated politicians cling to power even as their populations cry out for democracy, civil rights, and a brighter future. But as Russia still sees the region as within its sphere of influence, and has shown willingness to go to war with these countries over it, the will of the people is all too often overruled. Oh, and need I note that wars are still ongoing in Yemen, Syria, and Afghanistan, even as the US calls it quits in this chronically-troubled country?

An evermore assertive and aggressive China is at least fairly transparent about its long-term strategic objectives. The world's second-largest economy sees itself as the world's "Middle Kingdom," which was overtaken and (in its eyes) humiliated by other powers for centuries. Beijing now intends to take what it believes is its rightful place in the world—military and economic superpower status, full dominance of the Asia/Pacific region, and massive influence everywhere else.

China believes its continuous 4,000-year civilization makes it both the world's oldest and most natural top power, so it regards its rise as a return to the natural order of things. Foreign affairs students worldwide still read military strategist Sun Tzu's *The Art of War*, written during ancient times. As I mentioned earlier, some 500 years ago China had the world's largest economy, capital city, and even oceangoing navy. Legendary Admiral Zheng He and his "Treasure Fleet" belong to a time when China had some 3,500 exceptionally large wooden ships that dwarfed anything Europeans could even imagine in both size and number. But when Zheng died, all the ships were burned to ashes, as China turned in on itself and stagnated. Now China wants its top-class navy back, and is well on its way to building and training one so powerful that it already flashes amber to those who walk the corridors of the Pentagon and the defense ministries of America's allies. In fact, China's navy has surpassed America's in size to become the world's largest, if not yet the most powerful.

As we've seen, China is ready to play hardball with its neighbors, or indeed with any country. If China believes Hong Kong is not falling into line as it prescribes patriotic Chinese should, it is fully prepared to pare back Hong Kong's traditional liberties, as it is already doing. The civil disorder and widespread concern among Hong Kongers today leads many to question whether China will keep faith with its previous solemn commitments and make good on the promise of Britain's last governor of Hong Kong, Lord Patten. On that memorable handover day in 1997, Governor Patten pledged from that day forward the people of Hong Kong would run Hong Kong, asserting "that's the promise, and that's the unshakeable destiny."

And, indeed, I remember the great sense of promise on that day when my wife and I had the good fortune to be hosted by one of Hong Kong's most successful businessmen to witness the elaborate and historic handover celebrations. Imagine the pageantry and pomp of the British Empire commingled with the deep cultural traditions and ceremony of the world's oldest civilization. There wasn't a dry eye—or dry "anything," for that matter—on that rain-soaked night on June 30, when, just before the stroke of midnight, the Union Jack was lowered with one last playing of "God Save the Queen," followed by a 12-second interval before China's five-starred red flag was hoisted high above the viewing stands to the tune of the Chinese "March of the Volunteers." A who's who of global figures from over 40 countries witnessed this historic event, led by a star-studded UK delegation including Prince Charles; former British Prime Minister Margaret Thatcher; her successor, Tony Blair; and China's top tier, led by Chinese President Jiang Zemin and Premier Li Peng. History will judge whether the pomp and promise of that night will be vindicated. At this juncture it looks more like "one country, *one* system" is emerging—China's plan all along?

China's reach goes far beyond its neighbors, however. A PEN America report and research from the Council on Foreign Relations show that China's censors have influenced Hollywood productions to such an extent over the years that entertainers have begun making content that they know will appease Beijing, out of fear that failure to do so will exclude them from a massive market. Similarly, when Daryl Morey, then manager of the Houston Rockets, tweeted in support of the Hong Kong protests in 2019, the backlash from China was so great—with the Chinese Basketball Association even suspending cooperation with the Rockets—that the NBA put out a statement calling the tweet "regrettable," which in turn prompted outrage from US politicians like Senator Ted Cruz, former presidential candidate Beto O'Rourke, and former secretary of Housing and Urban Development Julián Castro. As journalist Matthew Yglesias notes, instead of becoming more democratic in the last 20 years, China appears to have just become better at exporting its censorship by using its economic clout to influence free speech abroad.

And China's military and naval hard power is already so potent that it's not clear the United States could prevail militarily in, for example, the South China Sea, should a confrontation boil over in this volatile environment.

US–China relations have seen better days. Trade angst, military anxieties, heightening technological competition . . . the two countries have plenty to argue about. Technology piracy, especially of hardware, has become a theater of these tensions as concerns of intellectual property theft and spying mount. Numerous Western politicians, including US legislators and UK intelligence chiefs, see their advanced technologies at risk at the hands of China. American lawmakers on both sides of the aisle, for instance, have expressed support for laws that support domestic semiconductor manufacturing out of fears of overreliance on Chinese imports and intellectual property theft.

No wonder various Western countries, cajoled by the US, are wary of using Chinese tech giant Huawei for their move to 5G networks. And, speaking of hardball, following Canada's detention of Huawei's CFO for possible extradition to the United States on criminal charges, China detained two Canadian citizens and charged them with espionage, even offering to "exchange" them for Huawei's CFO. Some might call that hostage taking with the offer of a quid pro quo.

Several years ago, my colleagues at Kearney and I predicted the rise of what we dubbed "multi-localism," which was already taking place before the pandemic and issues of national security came to the fore. Companies have always faced a tradeoff between the great cost efficiencies of running lean, just-in-time global supply chains and the risks that such operations could be disrupted or even severed by myriad unforeseen events, as we've seen with COVID-19. The direction for business operations now is toward localization, diversification, and reshoring to provide a higher level of security and resilience. Governments also risk relying too heavily on Chinese suppliers, not least for sensitive technologies that have national security implications. Semiconductors, for instance, have become a focal point of these anxieties as US officials look to reshore production, as have seemingly innocuous social media apps like TikTok. Who would've thought that an app that people use to post vacuous videos of themselves dancing or singing would become a flashpoint of US national security and relations with China?

Down under, these same issues are very much on the minds of Australian leaders, who seek to combine national security with a continued robust Chinese trading relationship, which has been tested during numerous recent disputes. Few people think of Australia as a rising military powerhouse, but it's spending tens of billions of dollars to counter and deter what it considers the growing Chinese threat in the Pacific. Though Australia has a population of only around 25 million people, it's making one of the world's largest purchases of F-35 Joint Strike Fighters for the Royal Australian Air Force—up to 100 planes, at more than US $100 million each, a price tag befitting the most advanced and stealthy fighter jet in aviation history. Its fast-growing fleet of new ships might well make the Royal Australian Navy larger than the onetime "mother service" of bygone days, Britain's Royal Navy. And Australia isn't doing all this out of a strutting militarism, but rather because it perceives the fast-changing geostrategic chessboard in its neighborhood, with lurking risks and dangers. In response to Australia's pushback against its strong-arm tactics in the Asia/Pacific region, China has begun boycotting a wide range of Australian goods, from copper ore and coal to wine, as a way of ratcheting up the economic pressure on a country that has come to depend on China as its main export market.

Australia is also working with the US, Japan, and another extremely important regional player—India—to revive the "Quad," the Quadrilateral Security Dialogue initiated by Prime Minister Shinzo Abe in

2007. All four countries, not least India, have grown more concerned about China's aggressiveness. Japan itself has expressed interest in a "Six Eyes" intelligence alliance (uniting Japan with the "Five Eyes" group of Australia, Canada, New Zealand, the US, and the UK) to mitigate and address the Chinese threat. Although India may appear to have lagged economically and in other ways compared with China, it, too, is a rising colossus—"The Tiger," if you will—one of immense economic, geopolitical, and military importance. Besides fielding one of the world's largest armies, India is showing emerging prowess in key Fourth Industrial Revolution technology by leveraging both its large population and its growing pool of highly educated people to fashion itself as a world leader in such future tech. With the most university-level graduates worldwide and over 2.6 million STEM graduates as of 2016, India's future looks bright and its technical capabilities only likely to grow. Beyond this, the Tiger and the Dragon comprise nearly 40 percent of the world's population—surely a force to consider.

Kishore Mahbubani, Singapore's brilliant thinker and doer, isn't so sure that the US and its allies are on track to deter or contain China. The author of *Has China Won?*, Kishore notes the two sides "eye each other warily across the Pacific; they communicate poorly; there seems to be little natural empathy; a massive geopolitical contest has begun." However, he believes that, in contrast to the US–Soviet rivalry, China has the edge. Unlike in the pre-1989 world, he feels, the United States is the power that has become inflexible, ideological, and systemically challenged, while China is adaptable, pragmatic, and strategic, much as the US once was.

By contrast, billionaire business figure and ideas entrepreneur Nicolas Berggruen and his right-hand thought leader Nathan Gardels, both of the LA-based Berggruen Institute, have quipped that, in their view, "China must lighten up, and the US must tighten up." And my aforementioned peers at the Center for Strategic and International Studies note that the United States could strengthen its position vis-à-vis China by building the skills of its workers so that they can compete in a global economy while organizing a "compact of the willing," or allies that could work together to think through global economic trading rules that work for everyone.

Russia, in comparison with China, is something of an enigma, even for veteran Kremlin watchers. Humiliated by the collapse of the USSR, only partially de-Sovietized, and accustomed to centuries of autocratic strongman rule, Russia appears to lack the long-term strategy of China, even if it has rebuilt its military hard power under Vladimir Putin, who has now positioned himself, much as China's Xi, as a ruler for life.

Russia can't aspire to the sort of "greatness" that is within China's grasp. Its economy, still largely dependent on oil and gas, has flatlined, and its demographics show a vast and largely empty country on a downward slope. Even its iconography still conjures the Soviet era, with the hammer and sickle or the red star imagery paired with revived Romanoff symbols such as the two-headed imperial eagle and tricolor flag.

However, Russia's intelligence services—honed by decades of KGB experience—are highly skilled, and Putin knows how to play the spoiler and stir up trouble with every form of "hybrid warfare," not least cyber. Nobody's better at using the latest techniques to interfere in other countries' elections, or at using the full range of ever-expanding tradecraft tools to try to undermine and destabilize the very social foundation of those societies. Russia's been investing massively in upgrading the technical abilities of its armed forces, so much so that numerous assessments and wargaming exercises have shown Russia having the upperhand in military conflicts in Eastern Europe *vis-à-vis* many Western adversaries. The discovery in late 2020 of a vast Russian hacking operation that allowed long-undetected backdoor entry into some 250 US federal government entities and major corporations was both jaw-dropping and frightening in its implications. This particularly audacious Russian intelligence operation was, if not formally an act of war, an attack upon the United States and a worrisome harbinger of future security threats.

Russia, of course, has been at this for decades. During my days at SRI International (the former Stanford Research Institute), we were managing the only official academic exchange with the then–Soviet

Union (during the Reagan era of heightened US–USSR tensions). Once a year we would lead a US delegation that traveled to the Soviet Union for "exchanges" with the Soviet Academy of Sciences; we would also host Soviet academicians in the US. While in Moscow we always knew we were being closely observed. It became a bit of a game to arrange personal items in your suitcase so that, on returning to one's hotel room at the end of a long day, you could determine how thoroughly your bag had been examined in your absence. And then, of course, there were the women of the night who would call in the wee hours to see if you wanted "company"—sometimes just offering their wares for money, but more often than not a honeytrap organized to film and photograph you in a compromising situation. The US, of course, returned the favor in a more obvious and respectable way, with the CIA reliably encamped on my office doorstep to inquire about my visit upon my return.

In theory, Russia has plenty of soft power at its disposal, including some of the greatest literature ever produced, unparalleled culture like the opera and ballet, and the world's endless fascination with the Romanoffs. Its language is one of the world's most widely spoken, and the vast country has a long history of collaboration and coexistence—not merely friction and conflict—with both Eastern and Western powers. This collaboration has benefited many more than just Russia. I'd rather not think about what our world might look like had Russia, the United Kingdom, and the United States not teamed up to beat Hitler during the Second World War. Those days of "Allied" partnership and collaboration are ancient history now. Instead, under Putin, Russia has preferred to trample upon international norms, disrespect the sovereignty of its neighbors, and stir up fear rather than win friends, despite the fact that sanctions and pariah status prove costly to Russia. Even non-NATO, peace-loving Sweden is beefing up defense spending as Russia becomes more aggressive. Some countries would rather be feared than loved, it seems.

I also got to know post-Soviet Russia well, having worked there as a strategy consultant both before and mostly after the fall of the Berlin Wall. One of my friends was the dynamic liberal reformer Boris Nemtsov, who did a stint as Russia's deputy prime minister, among many other roles. I met him in the early 1990s, when he was still the very young, visionary governor of Nizhny Novgorod (called "Gorky" during the Soviet period), one of the USSR's "closed science cities." It was a bit of a thrill to be one of the first Westerners to set foot in this formerly secret Russian Los Alamos. Boris had more than a touch of greatness about him, but ultimately he wasn't aligned with the new direction of Russian politics under Putin and went into open opposition. Tragically, and some believe inevitably, in 2015, he was assassinated in cold blood in Moscow near the Kremlin and Red Square, a murder still officially deemed "unsolved."

Another colleague has been Grigory Yavlinsky, who made critical contributions to liberalizing Russia's post-Communist economy. Grigory's enemies also made his life, and that of his family, difficult—they even kidnapped his 23-year-old pianist son in 1994, cut off three of his fingers, and mailed them home. And such violence long predates Putin's Russia of today. Six of the last twelve reigning tsars were murdered, showing that high office in Russia has always been a risky occupation. And forget about joining the opposition now, given the very real risk of being poisoned. The most recent example is of course Alexei Navalny, whose peril began with a failed assassination attempt in late 2020.

Star academic, author, and thinker Niall Ferguson believes we are already well into "Cold War II." We must ensure this war doesn't turn hot, and that a renewed international order can find ways to bring China and Russia inside the tent, as it were—with enough give-and-take to incentivize their participation in the global system, versus remaining adversaries with grievances they proclaim intractable.

Ferguson also has a suggestion for the US government: just as the president has a Council of Economic Advisors, a National Security Council, and other such bodies, he advocates the White House create a "Council of Historical Advisors." It's an interesting notion, as arguably too many US foreign policy decisions in recent decades have been made without an adequate consideration and deep knowledge of the history, culture, and geography of the regions they will affect. George W. Bush's White House could have used such a body profitably before venturing into interminable wars in Iraq and Afghanistan, given its misunderstandings of what was possible or achievable. (Ferguson, ever the interesting commentator, predicted in the immediate wake of the US Capitol being stormed that the majority of Americans would develop "herd immunity" against Trumpism as a result of that outrage . . . time will tell.)

Joe Joffe—German newspaper editor and Stanford fellow—has studied periods when new powers are rising and found them to be dangerous and risky times for the world. Consider the rise of Imperial Germany and Imperial Japan over a century ago, and how that ended. Joe says that countries growing in power sometimes behave like teenagers: testing limits, flexing their muscles, and driving too fast. The status quo powers rarely do a good job of accommodating such newcomers or finding ways to bring them under the tent of any existing international order. In looking at China today, we would do well to study the mistakes and missteps of the last time major new powers were bursting onto the world scene, in the period before 1914. By that August, it was already too late, and the world was set on a terrible path that would include two world wars, various revolutions, some 100 million deaths worldwide, and a Cold War that didn't end until 1989. Even now, the scars aren't fully healed.

In the meantime, while we try as best we can to bring China and Russia back as responsible participants in a renewed international order, we hope that deterrence will work as well in the Second Cold War as it worked in the first. During the first one—which, again, happily never turned "hot"—much of the war was waged through intelligence efforts. Today, Western intelligence and security services are working in overdrive to keep up with their Chinese and Russian counterparts. But it's more Silicon Valley than James Bond: technology, particularly in the areas of eavesdropping and surveillance (signals intelligence, or SIGINT), has become key. What was once a totally secret postwar intelligence alliance of the United States, United Kingdom, Canada, Australia, and New Zealand was revealed a few years ago as the Five Eyes network, and it remains at the top of the game, for now anyway.

Edward Lucas, intelligence expert, journalist, and senior vice president of the Center for European Policy Analysis, says that "technical expertise, rather than human sleuthing, will hold the key to future success." In Edward's view, old-school human intelligence (HUMINT) spycraft involving fake cover identities and false passports is increasingly difficult to sustain. Never mind the advances to come—even current facial recognition software, location tracing, and AI-enabled deep online research can blow the now-flimsy and manufactured cover of intelligence operatives very quickly, if not instantly. No wonder information-gathering technologies, particularly those that touch these national security and intelligence matters, are increasingly top of mind for policymakers.

As for other intelligence efforts, this one sounds like a joke: "A Dane, a Swede, a German, and a Dutchman walk into a bar . . . " Actually, in the 1970s, senior intelligence officials from these four countries met in a Munich-area bar, looking for a name for their new secret intelligence-sharing alliance, which they called Maximator, named after the locally-brewed Doppelbock beer they drank that night. France joined Maximator in 1985, but the very existence of the Maximator alliance was only revealed in spring 2020. Apart from Maximator and the even more potent Five Eyes, there are the Fourteen Eyes (officially SIGINT Seniors Europe), which brings together the Five Eyes and Maximator countries with Spain, Norway, Belgium, and Italy. And, as mentioned, there's been talk of adding Japan to the Five Eyes alliance, given grave worries about China, to make it the Six Eyes.

Many reasonable people have legitimate concerns about these eavesdropping and intelligence alliances, as there is always the potential they will invade citizens' privacy in the course of their normal business, which is not publicly accountable. As AI advances, this tension between freedom and privacy on the one hand and the "defence of the realm" (as the Brits call it) on the other, will become more acute. Such are the dilemmas we face in trying to keep the peace in Cold War II.

Retired US Navy admiral James Stavridis, who served as NATO's Supreme Allied Commander Europe, and later as dean of the Fletcher School of Law and Diplomacy, is now considered one of the West's most far-sighted thinkers on geostrategic issues, something I can attest to from our many interactions around the table with other global thought leaders. It is well known that Hillary Clinton considered him as a possible running mate in 2016, and that after Trump won, he was seen as a possible secretary of state. Today he views the global security landscape as mind-blowingly complex, lurking with dangers big and small, and with technological changes a key driving force in military matters—including AI, robotics, autonomous systems, cyber, and biowarfare. He foresees humans largely being taken out of the combat decision loop, as cars, drone aircraft, heavy land vehicles, surface ships, and submarines increasingly become "driverless platforms."

As far as AI goes, Jim states, "an entirely different level of AI will drive 'swarm' systems that can put hundreds or thousands of sensors or weapons to use in an autonomous fashion. The fusion of AI and mechanical systems will ultimately produce something akin to the human-like robots Isaac Asimov imagined 70 years ago in *I, Robot*. It will also bring to reality some of the frightening combat technology depicted in Peter Singer and August Cole's 2015 novel *Ghost Fleet*, in which swarming insect-sized sensing/killing machines flood the battlefield and knock out large enemy systems."

He goes on to say that the technologies we now rely on ("Yay, I can open my garage door from a thousand miles away!") also create "an enormous 'threat surface' through which malicious state actors, hacktivists and cyber-criminals can operate." He adds, "Defense satellites will be used for counter-space operations (attacking other satellites) and commercial disruption . . . [and] if the coronavirus pandemic has taught us nothing else, it is that we should respect the potential for biology to change all of our lives in an instant." As a result, he argues, bioweapon development will doubtless accelerate.

Meanwhile, our militaries will rely more on commandos and special forces rather than large, mass armies, which are costly to maintain and easy targets for malicious actors. Such special forces will have elite training and be equipped with advanced gear. He explains: "Shadowy teams of highly skilled operators will link together . . . immediate access to satellite-provided precision information, calling on autonomous attack platforms, using cyberwarfare programs to confuse and disrupt the enemy, and relying on human performance enhancements to sustain themselves over long tactical periods. Russian 'hybrid warfare' which was used so effectively on Ukraine and Georgia was a nascent version of this."

Remember Russian bots retweeting disinformation and fake news? Even if still widely used, they're so yesterday. Today's advances in video and audio editing technology allow the creation of weaponized deep-fake videos so uncannily real that they can leave you completely fooled. For an example of this, go to YouTube to watch President Richard Nixon's televised address to the nation announcing the sad failure of the Apollo 11 moon landing and the death of Neil Armstrong and his fellow astronauts. His speechwriters did prepare such an address in the event of mission failure, but happily it never needed to be delivered. However, current technology allows you to watch Nixon deliver that message, and it's bone-chilling to realize how a broadcast that never happened could be so skillfully faked from scratch. The technology is also expanding to create fake faces and images of individuals that foreign agencies use to connect with government employees and steal information. Mark Twain is said to have quipped, "A lie can travel halfway around the world while the truth is putting on its shoes." Never was that truer than today.

So while we in the US do what is urgently needed to address the four existential threats (public health risks and inadequate healthcare, corrosive inequality, racial injustice, and climate change) challenging the very viability of our democracy, we must do so while keeping a close eye on the needs and challenges presented by the world's other major players.

America needs to re-engage as a leader in the rules-based international order again. While the post-Bretton Woods international order surely needs reform, the United States cannot afford to be a no-show in the global arena. Here, in 2016, the countries of the world, convened by the United Nations, adopted the Paris Climate Accord—to which the United States renewed its commitment in 2021.

CHAPTER NINE

IT'S ALSO TIME FOR A "GLOBAL NEW DEAL" THAT RESTORES THE INTERNATIONAL ORDER

> "Paradoxically—the process of globalization tempts
> a nationalism that threatens its fulfillment."
> —HENRY KISSINGER

Now that I may well have scared you about the state of our world, I'd like to offer a more positive vision of foreign affairs. I hope I have made the case that America needs a *New* New Deal that reinvigorates our government and makes the most of our can-do spirit. But we shouldn't stop there. Our world is so interconnected that we need to ensure that anything we do at home is done with awareness and sensitivity to the world around us. Likewise, what happens beyond our borders impacts us directly, and sometimes immediately, as we've seen only too well. The biggest questions of our day—public health, equitably shared prosperity, managing climate change, and racial justice—are not only connected (and therefore need to be addressed comprehensively), but also do not respect borders. We can no longer consider domestic policy and foreign policy separate, unrelated domains. That's why I'm making the case for a Global New Deal that renews and restores the international order, inspired by our past but refreshed to build a better future.

Any such effort, while critical, will involve so many countries, institutions, conflicting interests, and moving parts that it is beyond the scope of this book to offer up a very detailed set of prescriptions. But the key to advancing a global reform agenda is ensuring America re-engages with the world as a leader and trusted partner after the Trump years of being perceived as an erratic bully.

I've talked a lot about US inequality in this book, but we should not forget that rising discrepancies between rich and poor are not a uniquely American problem. An Organisation for Economic Co-operation and Development (OECD) study found that, across a broad range of countries, median incomes (essentially those of the middle class) grew much slower between 1985 and 2015 than incomes among the top 10 percent of earners. Another OECD study found that the share of income going to the top 1 percent in a number of countries—including ones not known for massive wealth inequalities, like the Netherlands and Denmark—was higher in 2016 than 1997. A number of emerging markets, like India, Brazil, and many African countries, also struggle with inequality. Unfortunately, the pandemic only made matters worse, increasing food insecurity and unemployment just as incomes fell. Since many of us are grappling with the same issues, we'll be more likely to address these issues effectively if we do so collaboratively.

So, where's the "global" part in my *New* New Deal? Most of my proposals in chapter seven require action at the level of the nation-state, because that's how we're structured—despite the fact that the world's most vexing problems leap over national borders. But it's a fact that the post-1945 international order is tattered, with many of the world's key international bodies and treaty organizations long dysfunctional and badly needing institutional transformation. Furthermore, the United States has retreated from its traditional global leadership role in recent years. Andrew Imbrie, author of *Power on the Precipice,* put it this way: "America's [relative] decline today is about one superpower at war with itself, even as other states are rising and gaining in stature." Fortunately the Biden administration is working fast to make up for this lagging pace.

The European Union, a far-sighted alliance intended (in the words of the organizing 1950 Schuman Declaration) to make the lunacy of another world war "not merely unthinkable, but materially impossible," has lost, through Brexit, its second biggest economic member—in my view, to the detriment of both Britain and the EU.

China and Russia don't feel what's left of the rules-based postwar international order is consistent with their national interests, so they have been doing their best to accelerate its demise. This shouldn't surprise us, as we are living off the fumes of the Bretton Woods system, which emerged after delegates from over 40 nations, huddled in the Mount Washington Hotel in Bretton Woods, New Hampshire, matched minds and wills for just over three weeks in July 1944. There they crafted a new international order and sketched out new international bodies and programs. For decades, those institutions were able to inspire and engage a war-weary "never again" world. But what was once visionary urgently needs to be remade in the context of a radically changed global reality. Some UN bodies are indeed zombie institutions now, ineffective and straying from their purpose.

As Moisés Naím told me, "The multilateral world of international institutions tends to be very inefficient. It's very easy to make fun of it. But if it didn't exist, we would need to invent it again. And in that new invention, we would require the nations that 'own' these institutions and control them to behave more responsibly and more globally, and not put their short-term electoral preferences and priorities as obstacles to a job that has to be done effectively and technically."

To create such shared stakes, a global financial transaction tax, very small in percentage terms but massive in cumulative monies raised, could underwrite the cost of a Global New Deal for the world. Researchers at the Austrian Institute for Economic Research estimate that such a tax could bring in billions of revenue annually, equal to 0.43 percent of global GDP. We need a global all-party agreement to craft this new prescription, which a traumatized "never again" post–COVID-19 world community should be more ready to accept than at any time in living memory. Again, as with other proposals I have advanced herein, the design specifications of this tax are beyond the scope of this book. I am simply trying to demonstrate the urgent need, compelling purpose, and practical application of such an initiative for which the technical policy-making expertise could easily be mobilized.

Addressing the pandemic, Margaret MacMillan of the University of Toronto put it this way in May 2020: "People coming out of a calamity are open to sweeping changes . . . We face a choice: to build better ways of dealing domestically and internationally with [these challenges] or let our world become meaner and more selfish, divided, and suspicious."

Henry Kissinger, now approaching 100 years old but mentally sharp as ever, also urges thinking big, literally in terms of a new Marshall Plan or Manhattan Project. In early April 2020 he wrote in the *Wall Street Journal* that "the coronavirus pandemic will forever alter the world order . . . The pandemic has prompted an anachronism, a revival of the walled city in an age when prosperity depends on global trade and movement of people . . . Now, we live in an epochal period. The historic challenge for leaders is to manage the crisis while building the future."

Building the future requires specific ideas and policies, not just broad calls for action. An example? I've written elsewhere about the Charter City idea developed by Nobel Prize–winning economist Paul Romer, and it remains an intriguing if still untried concept. The idea is that if country X is an ungovernable mess, no one can possibly take on reforming the whole country. But maybe it's just possible to carve out a small area—a kind of new city-state or special autonomous zone—and make sure everything works properly, from the justice system to infrastructure and education to public services and neighborhood safety. The troubled country of Honduras originally agreed to try a Charter City experiment in 2012, but it got tangled up in domestic legal and constitutional problems. As I've said before, it's hard to create a new Silicon Valley from scratch (almost all such attempts have failed), but what about one or more new Hong Kongs, Dubais, or Singapores? Romer, by the way, was the person who coined the phrase, "a crisis is a terrible thing to waste."

Saudi Arabia is well aware that the age of oil is coming to a close, and with their Vision 2030 and other strategic plans, the Kingdom is trying to prepare for life beyond petrodollars. The country has some 80 mega-projects underway, including "Neom," a futuristic mega-city some 33 times larger than New York on the Red Sea coast, with artificial rain, robotic maids, and holographic teachers. It will also be home to the world's largest hydrogen project, which will run on solar and wind power and produce up to 650 tons of hydrogen daily, showing how forward-thinking its plans are. In line with the Charter City concept, it will have its own autonomous legal structure and jurisdiction.

Another twist on this idea comes from Dr. Christian Kälin, who founded what is now officially called the "investment migration" industry as well as its leading firm, Henley & Partners—the first stop for those rich people, often from troubled countries, who seek a new home base and even a new nationality. Henley pioneered citizenship- and residence-by-investment; although both the industry and its leading light are not without controversy, Henley has encouraged regulation of the sector to make it respectable and ensure that crooks can't just buy a new citizenship and passport. As the market leader, Kälin's firm has a philanthropic arm, the Andan Foundation, that is putting a new twist on the Charter City idea by linking it to the problems of refugees fleeing war zones and to international migration pressures more generally. They ask why we can't carve out mini, Hong Kong–style Charter Cities for refugees and desperate migrants who want to work hard and rebuild their lives, located in countries with suitable open space—also thereby taking the migration pressure off Europe. Worth a shot? Just think of the creative energy that could be unleashed when persecuted people are able to think freely and ambitiously about their future and those of their loved ones and communities. After all, the United States was founded as a refuge for oppressed people seeking a free and fresh start, and look how far an immigration-based development trajectory has taken us!

Another newcomer to the Charter City movement is Milton Friedman's grandson, Patri Friedman, a former Google software engineer who has formed Pronomos Capital to raise venture funding and start launching experimental Charter Cities in vacant areas of developing countries that are willing to give the idea a try. Such deep-pocketed Silicon Valley figures as Peter Thiel and Marc Andreesen have already given Pronomos seed money, and it appears several countries, including Ghana, the Marshall Islands, Nigeria, Panama, and even Honduras, whose prior attempt didn't get off the ground, might be game. Given their relative poverty and the many challenges they face, these countries may be more willing than most to experiment with these kinds of untested, if arguably high-potential, pilot projects.

The Charter City concept is characteristic of many such efforts to "wire around" the nonfunctional aspects of the international system without reforming existing multilateral institutions. Unsurprisingly, many countries consider overhauling the Bretton Woods institutions as an impossible task, and so look to create other work-arounds through new and separate, often regional, initiatives that bypass the postwar bodies altogether.

One example is Europe's Three Seas Initiative, a forum of 12 countries bordering the Baltic, Adriatic, and Black seas. The leaders of these nations first met in 2016 in Dubrovnik, Croatia, and current plans include big-ticket energy and transport projects, including a €6 billion Rail Baltica project linking Warsaw to Estonia's capital Tallinn, and a North–South highway dubbed the "Via Carpathia" going from the Lithuanian port city of Klaipeda to Thessaloniki in Greece. Time will tell whether the Three Seas Initiative will realize its big ambitions or fade into a regional talking shop.

Other regional European groupings range from the relatively tight Visegrád Four alliance (Poland, Hungary, the Czech Republic, and Slovakia) in Central Europe to the Nordic-Baltic 8, joining together the Scandinavian and Baltic countries, which regard themselves as sharing such "Northern" cultural values as social solidarity, fiscal responsibility, and low levels of corruption.

The newcomer to this scene is the recently founded Lublin Triangle of Poland, Lithuania, and Ukraine. Bringing into closer contact three nations that were historically linked in one polity for centuries, the Triangle seeks to integrate Ukraine more closely with Europe and defend it from Russian irredentism and aggression. On that note, Poland is arguably the great success story of the post-Soviet bloc, a relatively large country of nearly 40 million people that has been enjoying a long economic boom and increasing influence as a "middle power" located at a strategic crossroads between East and West. Yet many are baffled by its embrace of prickly populist-nationalist politics, especially since Poles are notably individualistic, freedom-loving, and pro-American. The paradox is at least partly explained by the country's traumatic and at times tragic history, which continues to affect the still-raw national psyche.

Another, if very different, possible alliance is something called CANZUK, which has stoked some interest given Britain's exit from the EU. Originally conceived in the 1960s before the UK joined what was then still called the European Economic Community, the CANZUK idea is to forge a union for mutual defense, free trade, and free movement of people embracing the UK, Canada, Australia, and New Zealand.

Critics, however, dismiss it as a nostalgic, post-Imperial, Union Jack–waving Anglosphere fantasy, long past its sell-by date. Whatever arrangement, if any, is struck, Britain will still trade mostly with Europe, Canada with the United States, and Australia with Asia.

Whether or not CANZUK, the Three Seas Initiative, or other regional integration schemes are ultimately successful in their goals, they tell us that many countries have largely given up on what's left of the Bretton Woods system, deeming global multilateral institutions and arrangements as deadwood that is nearly impossible to reform. Certainly, a number of international bodies are stagnant, clapped-out institutions, but they live on with big budgets and bureaucracies. As for regional groupings, few have managed to maintain the momentum of their founding periods, though perhaps ASEAN anchored by Singapore and its neighbors still represents something of a success story.

Africa also looks like a region set for further integration as the continent enjoys the benefits of the recently ratified African Continental Free Trade Area (AfCFTA). The World Bank estimates that the pact could add $450 billion to the continent in cumulative potential income by 2035, and lift 30 million people out of extreme poverty. Cyril Ramaphosa, South Africa's highly capable president (even if politically challenged by the daunting problems he inherited from the corrupt leadership of his predecessor), has spoken eloquently of the compelling need to harness regional resources. I got to know and collaborate with Cyril when he founded the country's highly successful investment holding firm, Shanduka. We (Kearney and Shanduka) jointly established the first wholly African-owned management consulting firm, Fever Tree, which continues to this day. On one occasion during a pre-pandemic visit to South Africa to discuss the implications for Africa of the Fourth Industrial Revolution, Cyril understood instantly that the only way Africa can hope to leverage these new technologies was through cross-regional collaborative initiatives. Cyril proclaimed to me, "We in Africa missed the first three industrial revolutions. We can't afford to miss this one."

I'm not sure I can say that the leaders of South America's Mercosur or Andean Community, never mind the Caribbean's CARICOM, have the same clarity of vision. NAFTA, now reborn as the USMCA, recently survived what appeared to be a close shave with extinction. Here, again, programs designed to meet different needs at different points in history need to be restructured in light of current reality. I got my first close look at regional economic integration schemes as a young professional working with the United Nations on a comparative assessment of the Andean Pact and the East African Economic Union. What worked then in those two needy regions of the world clearly doesn't work now. The needs are greater than ever, but the institutional frameworks have not evolved and grown to meet those needs.

Pope Francis once said, "Reforming Rome is like cleaning the Sphinx of Egypt with a toothbrush." You could say much the same about the UN system, or about the broader collection of multilateral and intergovernmental bodies that have grown up somewhat haphazardly over decades.

At one point there were high hopes for the G20—the Group of Twenty—which was founded in 1999 to further global financial stability but in principle is an ideal grouping for tackling world crises like a pandemic. Made up of 19 key countries plus the European Union as the 20th member, the G20 represents some 90 percent of gross world product, 80 percent of world trade, and two-thirds of the world's population. Its annual summits of heads of state and government, as well as of finance ministers and central bank governors, always make for good photo ops, if not always substantive progress. On COVID-19, unfortunately, the G20 was essentially a no-show. Although many international organization bureaucracies are infamous for their administrative bloat, that the G20 has so far decided not to create a permanent secretariat may be a weakness for a global body that seeks to respond decisively to big issues, including breaking crises. I see the G20 as a body with considerable unrealized promise, and one worth building on.

Kishore Mahbubani, the provocative thinker and straight-talking Singaporean leader who served as his country's ambassador to the UN, and was the founding dean of the Lee Kuan Yew School of Public Policy, also did two stints as president of the UN Security Council, and has been called "the Muse of the Asian Century." When I talked with Kishore last year about what can be done to renew our broken-down multilateral institutions, he had the following eye-opening things to say:

> You know, Paul, I think you've had more experience in helping to strengthen and build organizations than I have. But I think one thing that you and I will completely agree on is that if you were asked to rescue any organization, the first thing you would do is, let me find the most dynamic, capable, courageous CEO to run this organization. And when you talk about the weakness of the United Nations, and you talk about the weakness of the World Health Organization, I can tell you that the reason why they're weak, they're not weak by accident. They're weak by design.
>
> Because if you are a strong, dynamic, courageous CEO, you are *not* qualified to become Secretary General of the United Nations, because of the requirement of the five permanent members of the UN Security Council, where as you know, I served as president twice. They don't agree on everything, but one thing they agree on

is that when you select a UN Secretary General, you want somebody who's relatively spineless.

Now if you have a selection process, whereby only spineless people are to run an organization, why should you be surprised that the organization underperforms? What we have to do is change our mindset towards these organizations, and realize that the world will be better off if we have stronger CEOs for these organizations, and we must fund them well. So, at the end of the day, the solutions are actually quite simple and easy to find. But of course, first you have to make a political decision: yes, I want a courageous, principled, strong, dynamic individual to run an organization like the United Nations.

As you know, our late mutual friend Paul Volcker genuinely believed that in institutions of government, you must select the best and you must train them well. And I can tell you, the whole world would be very happy to see the return of a strong and dynamic United States of America, once again, leading the world with the same kind of generous spirit with which America led the world in the decades after World War II.

I recall that when Volcker was Chairman of the US Federal Reserve, he used to talk about America's three deficits: fiscal, trade, and talent. Of these three, he would assert the most worrisome was the government leadership talent deficit.

As I've said, whether we are speaking of relations between nations or between citizens, collaboration and solidarity—whether high or low—will also be a critical defining factor of the kind of culture and world we will experience. The pandemic should have sparked a new sense of solidarity and collaboration among peoples and countries "all in this together," but to date that has been sporadic. It remains to be seen whether the crisis will ultimately have been a catalyst for the kind of cooperative spirit all societies and the world as a whole so badly need, and whether the strategic rivalry involving the US, China, and Russia can be managed relatively peacefully, through a refashioned, rules-based international order. Such a new global system can work only if all players feel they have a stake in its success and are prepared to endow the leadership and rules of this system with "spine."

Whether we're dealing with inequality within our own societies or cooperation among countries, we have to realize that we're all on the same boat. Recent crises should be making that all the more clear. As Kishore also told me:

> If there's one big message from COVID-19 and its rapid spread, it confirms what I've said [earlier] . . . 7.5 billion people live in 193 separate countries. In the past, they used to live in 193 separate boats with captains and crews taking care of each boat and rules to make sure the boats didn't collide. But today as a result of globalization, and you can see this with COVID-19, the 7.5 billion people no longer live in 193 separate boats. They live in 193 separate cabins on the same boat. But the problem about a global boat is that you have captains and crews taking care of each cabin. And no captains or crews taking care of the global boat as a whole . . . So at some point, humanity has to wake up and understand that now we live literally on the same boat.

I wholeheartedly agree with Kishore. We're all on the same boat, and it's time that we realized that and worked together to make sure it operates smoothly. I believe it's time to leave behind the isolationist mentality that grew ever stronger during the Trump years. If we want to focus on domestic problems to achieve the much-coveted *All-American Comeback*, we need to do what we can to ensure global peace and prosperity. As Americans we should be incredibly proud that our country has been a global leader, helping shepherd some of humanity's greatest achievements, from new technologies to the creation of global institutions to beating both fascism and Soviet Communism. But we need to get our mojo back. We must turn our quintessentially American, optimistic, can-do pragmatism to the incredible challenges and opportunities that lie ahead of us, crying out for leadership. We can build a better country and world that will lift us all up and propel us into a brighter tomorrow. So let's roll up our sleeves and get to it!

We are not hostages to some preordained future. We must be enablers of the future we want for ourselves and our children. But to do so, we need to bring that future into focus and chart the necessary course to get us there. So let's act now to get it right.

AFTERWORD

AFTERWORD

by Dr. Moisés Naím, Distinguished Fellow, Carnegie Endowment for International Peace, Washington, DC

Pandemics remake the world. They always have.

In the year 541, from his base in Constantinople (current day Istanbul), the Eastern Roman emperor Justinian was on the verge of re-uniting the two halves of the Roman empire for the first time in nearly a century, driving back the Germanic tribes that had conquered Italy and re-establishing Rome as the Imperial capital. He had nearly succeeded, scoring victory after victory against the Goths, when a flea, having hitched a ride from Central Asia on the horse of one of the marauders that regularly came to pillage Europe at the time, bit his rider soldier and infected him with the *Yersinia pestis* bacterium.

The epidemic of plague that resulted ravaged the Eastern empire, killing—as best as today's historians can make out—somewhere between 25 and 60% of the people of Europe. Tens of millions died in this Plague of Justinian. The emperor himself contracted it in 542 but was one of the lucky few that survived. What did not survive was his life-long ambition to reunite the halves of the Roman Empire: the project to reconquer Italy from the Goths failed, the Western Empire crumbled, and Western Europe fell into the 1000-year torpor we now know as the Middle Ages.

Some 800 years later, the Black Death—another outbreak of *Yersinia pestis*—ravaged Europe again, the resulting mass death driving up the cost of labor throughout the continent and allowing for the creation of an incipient middle class of better off artisans and farmers who would, over the next century, become the material backbone that allowed the renaissance to develop. And 300 years after *that,* the outbreak of pandemic flu in the German trenches at the end of the Great War finally broke the Kaiser's army, giving rise to the punitive Peace of Versailles and setting the stage for the later tragedies in European history.

Plagues remake our cultural world as well, often in surprising ways. One bored Florentine writer, Boccaccio, whiled away the boredom of 14th century lockdown by writing the Decameron. Three centuries later another bored bard decided to pass the time during lockdown by writing a play—*King Lear.* Our common cultural heritage would be unrecognizable without pandemics.

That the 2020-2021 Coronavirus Pandemic would alter the course of history in permanent and profound ways is, then, the opposite of surprising. It's what we should expect, knowing what we do about what pandemics have done in the past. Pandemics shift our understanding of what's normal and of what's possible. They bury pre-pandemic sacred cows, alter pre-pandemic power relations, reconfigure the entire landscape of political, economic and social relations that result. Pandemics remake the world; they always have.

What's tricky is spotting the direction of travel right in the heat of the health crisis. No one could have foreseen, when that one flea bit that one horseman in 541, that the result would be almost a millennium of cultural stagnation. Few could have guessed, as city after city in 14th century Europe locked its gates in a doomed attempt to keep out the bubonic plague, that the convulsion would give rise, within a hundred years, to the greatest flourishing the human imagination had known in a thousand years. Plagues, as Albert Camus once wrote, are not made on a human scale. Their historical implications, I want to add, are similarly beyond us.

Yet Paul Laudicina is undoubtedly correct, in these pages, in spying in the Coronavirus Pandemic the makings of a unique historic opportunity. Because plagues have a curious way of making yesterday's impossibility into tomorrow's forgone conclusion, and yesterday's immutable reality into tomorrow's discarded dogma. Pandemics reshuffle the decks of human possibility, and today we are living through one of these rare, precious, terrifying, fraught and promising moments.

In the United States, astonishing transformations happened almost instantly. The CARES Act approving $2.2 trillion in relief spending, for instance, was approved by a *Republican* congress and signed into law by a *Republican* president a mere two weeks after the pandemic was declared. An entrenched ideological impossibility became a practical inevitability at a surprising speed. That's the power of pandemic—and the promise of the moment we now live in. And this book provides smart and practical ideas to help us navigate today's stormy waters.

In these pages, Laudicina has eloquently and usefully synthesized the transformational policy agenda required to engineer an *All-American Comeback*. A broad and deep reformist agenda is needed to marry equity with the potential of radical innovation, and this provocative and revealing book contains its key ingredients. Just as it took a 14th century pandemic to create the conditions for the European renaissance, we may look back on this 21st century pandemic as the prerequisite for building America's own renaissance. But this is no foregone conclusion. As the emperor Justinian found out, some pandemics cripple civilizational renewals instead of catalyzing them.

And there is plenty of reason for concern. The pandemic has shown that while the world's capacity for rapid innovation is undiminished and, frankly, awesome, the resources it takes to innovate are not equally distributed throughout society. While the scientific establishment rose to the challenge with astonishing creativity and technical prowess, compressing the time it takes to develop a new vaccine beyond what anyone thought possible, our governing institutions struggled to keep up. While scientific visionaries like Dr. Katalin Karikó, Dr. Ugur Sahin, and Dr. Özlem Türeci, pioneered entirely new forms of medicine based on Nanotech advances that were science fiction only a few years ago, governments plod along, responding to the crisis with legacy "technologies" such as the Unemployment Insurance, a U.S innovation that dates back to the Social Security Act of 1935.

The bold, inventive, ambitious scientists and the knowledge-based, disruptive corporations stand in sharp contrast against the gray, tradition-bound, unimaginative public sector and the politicians who control it. This contrast should serve as a big, bright warning sign of danger ahead. This imbalance, if not addressed, threatens to land America in the *Tech Lords Rule* scenario, with owners of new technologies (and big chunks of capital) hoarding nearly all the fruits of innovative growth. Worse, it could engender a populist backlash that punishes those tech titans and lands us squarely in *Dollar Store America*—a country that neither innovates nor includes. The scenarios developed by Paul Laudicina in this book provide excellent examples of the alternative futures that the United States is facing.

The times call for bold experimentation in government. Not just innovative policies, but also innovative ways of *making* policy. Ambitious trials of groundbreaking new ideas like Universal Basic Income are important, yes, but so are ambitious reforms to our election system, to our ways of discussing and adopting policy, and certainly to the way we finance politics in the United States.

The reality, today, is that Americans—and most other countries— are facing up to 21st century social problems using 20th century welfare state institutions, and when we try to reform those institutions, we do it with assumptions and mindsets that have not changed much since the 18th century.

In the United States our reverence for the Founding Fathers has served the country well. It has preserved political stability and cohesion through crises that might otherwise have spelled the end of the republic. Naturally, though, that's only one part of the story. The other side, often silenced, is a dearth of innovation when it comes to politics and governmental decision-making practices. It's as though we decided the last word on this was uttered in 1787, and no more needs to be said.

But much more needs to be said. Digital technologies and fifty years' worth of research in cognitive science and social psychology are upending what we know about the way we make decisions in almost every aspect of our lives. In almost all, except for one that is critical for our future: positive, democratic disruptive changes are not easy to find in the world of politics and governing. If policy-making remains a laggard in this respect, we can hardly expect very good policy to be made.

Indeed, there are promising experiments afoot, both in the US at state and local level and internationally. Alaska and Maine have both implemented ranked-choice voting, a method designed to weed out the type of extreme candidate with "deep but narrow" bases of support that can sneak into office when facing a divided field, as happened during the Republican presidential primaries in 2016. Ireland has brought together Citizen Juries, panels of 100 citizens selected at random to discuss controversial policy problems and propose consensus ideas, with great success. Brazil and Taiwan have experimented with online discussion platforms that ban anonymity and reward consensus building rather than shrill extremism.

Many more transformational ideas are out there, waiting for someone to give them a try. Some will succeed, others will fail. But if we're unwilling to reconsider the shape of these basic institutions in response to pandemic, we will be setting ourselves up for a future we should not wish to the next generations.

For business leaders, the temptation is to think they can just skip these sorts of political representation problems: hunker down, focus on your business, and hope the storm passes you by. But it isn't that simple. As the very high profile spat that in 2021 pitted Georgia's Republican party against the state's biggest companies following the adoption of a hyper-restrictive voting law shows, dysfunctional and outdated political institutions will eventually reach a level of rot that the C-suite can't afford to ignore. There's no opting out of the political instability that decayed institutions generate.

Another future is indeed possible. And history is a guide. In the 1350s, following the Black Death, the basic institutions of medieval society were rapidly transformed. Barbaric ancient institutions like serfdom died out, and the incipient early forerunners of modern labor unions, craft guilds, saw rapid growth as labor shortages increased the wages of town dwellers. Out of an appalling tragedy, a society that was better able to offer freedom and security to its humblest members was born.

We can do the same. And this book can help us do it.

ACKNOWLEDGMENTS

The COVID-19 pandemic has left many indelible marks on our collective psyche. Understandably, we tend to recall its negative impacts, which have engendered an almost primal sense of personal insecurity as the world struggled to comprehend and control this invisible threat to our physical well-being. The millions of infections and lives lost not only brought incredible pain and grief while disrupting our lives and livelihoods, but also inspired many to seek a deepened sense of community and common cause. And in the process, many of us have discovered a new sense of gratitude for those around us who every day provide us and those close to us, often invisibly, with what we need to live healthy, fulfilled, purpose-driven, and relatively friction-free lives.

I count myself among those fortunate few who were able to pull up the drawbridge and work from home with frequent (if remote) connection to family, friends, and colleagues, tapping the relationship equity I have from a lifetime of in-person connections. As noted in my Preface, this enforced physical isolation and "freedom" from extensive travel allowed for the reflection and electronic engagement that helped give life to this book. Even so, the pandemic significantly shifted the direction of this book from my original concept of imparting lessons learned over the course of my career from my engagement with leaders around the world.

The initial seed for that project was sown, actively encouraged, and supported by my long-standing colleague, intellectual partner, and dear friend, Erik Peterson, the very able and inspiring managing director of the Kearney Global Business Policy Council. So I need first and foremost to thank Erik for being my constant intellectual sparring partner throughout this whole journey. His creative insights and active involvement in all aspects of this book were not only central to my thinking, but also to my motivation to keep at this manuscript, even during the darkest days of pandemic-induced disruption.

Stephen Klimczuk was my copilot and alter ego in charting this "Roadmap to a Brighter Future," much as he was with my last two books. Without his guidance, intellectual breadth, depth of insight, engaged advocacy, and active pen from the very beginning of this project, I would never have been able to reimagine America's possibilities. He and I go back many years in the trenches together, helping clients across the globe rigorously research, powerfully imagine, and courageously embrace and enable more desirable futures than those that might otherwise emerge. I am eternally indebted to Stephen for continuing our partnership by bringing to this book his extraordinary intelligence, deep curiosity, insatiable energy, good humor, and broad-gauged knowledge.

Working with Stephen and me as co-architects of this book are three of Kearney's Global Business Policy Council's brightest stars. Terry Toland's fingerprints are all over this book's four visions of the future. He used his well-developed and time-tested skill as a scenario planner to help reimagine the alternative paths down which the US might be headed. Rebecca Grenham was as central to the book's background research as she was to enhancing the clarity and consistency of its narrative. And Emily Hazzard was incredibly creative and persistent in finding the best graphics to capture and enhance the book's substance and sentiment, as well as helping organize all of us through the many steps involved in book production in such a compressed period of time while managing the press of other business . . . all remotely.

The forced isolation of the pandemic offered me the bonus of many more hours with my wife and soul mate Louise, whom I have relied upon always to give me frank and unerringly correct counsel, not only on the substance of this book, but also on many of life's lessons noted herein, through which she had to suffer over many years, often vicariously.

My four children and their two spouses, Chris, Lee and Jo, Carla and Nick, and Nikki, also have kept me honest (and have at least tried to keep me humble) as I was distilling life's lessons into this volume, often while a pre-pandemic absentee dad. One of the special tortures of this extended period of social distancing is to have missed personally witnessing those once-in-a-lifetime early developmental stages of my two precious grand-children, Kenzie and Logan. My daughter Nikki, who, like so many of her peers, was forced to complete her undergraduate education remotely while at home with Louise and me, had the special misfortune of being subjected to (and invariably challenged on, as a Gen-Z'er should!) what undoubtedly must have seemed like interminable dinner discussions of all the key questions this book addresses.

I am deeply honored and especially grateful to my good friend and mentor Moisés Naím for writing what his many followers will recognize as a quintessentially insightful Afterword that only someone of his intel-lectual stature and creativity could pen. I count myself extremely fortu-nate to have benefitted so much from Moisés, as do countless millions of others around the world who have read his published insights, watched his TV interviews, delighted in his books and screenplays, or been in his audiences. To have had a front seat in those forums is special enough, but to count Moisés among my dearest personal friends is a special joy that has enriched my life and inspired me in so many ways.

As the reader will note, this book also benefits from the insights of many other thinkers and leaders across a broad swath of disciplines, geographies, and institutions, most of whom I have had the good for-tune of collaborating with over many years. They are too numerous to acknowledge by name here, but you have seen their wisdom in the broad spectrum of thought and inspiration that has leavened and influenced my thinking. I thank them collectively for continuing to inspire and motivate me, not least in writing this book.

Needless to say, beyond the close collaboration with my many partners, in writing this book I have benefitted immeasurably from a very talented and committed group of professionals working in this most challenging book market. I am grateful to my very experienced and wise literary agent Jeff Herman for believing in this project and helping put it on the right track . . . more than once, including finding the perfect publisher for this book. Matt Holt Books, led by Matt Holt, took a chance on this book when the future seemed quite glum for the world . . . and especially for book publishers. He, in turn, brought to the table a very talented graphic artist, Brigid Pearson, and an equally talented (and understanding) editor, Katie Dickman, without whose professional support this book would not have seen the light of day. Katie Hollister, our production associate, also deserves my hearty thanks.

Finally, mindful of the admonition of one of my former mentors that one should never "die with a secret," this book and the thoughts contained herein reaped incredible value from the book marketing firm Book Highlight. I am thankful to Mat Miller, Peter Knox, Brian Morrison, and Alana Whitman for believing in the thesis of this book and employing their special skills to ensure that the ideas and the insights contained herein help inspire my readers to embrace a brighter future by actively reimaging and realizing America's possibilities.

—PAL

SELECTED BIBLIOGRAPHY

Applebaum, Anne. *Twilight of Democracy: The Seductive Lure of Authoritarianism.* New York: Doubleday, 2020.

Berggruen, Nicolas, and Nathan Gardels. *Intelligent Governance for the 21st Century: A Middle Way Between West and East.* Cambridge, England: Polity, 2014.

Bodanis, David. *The Art of Fairness: The Power of Decency in a World Turned Mean.* London: Bridge Street Press, 2020.

Bregman, Rutger. *Humankind: A Hopeful History.* New York: Little, Brown, 2020.

Brooks, David. *Bobos in Paradise: The New Upper Class and How They Got There.* New York: Simon & Schuster, 2000.

Case, Anne, and Angus Deaton. *Deaths of Despair and the Future of Capitalism.* Princeton, NJ: Princeton University Press, 2020.

Christakis, Nicholas. *Apollo's Arrow: The Profound and Enduring Impact of Coronavirus on the Way We Live.* New York: Little, Brown Spark, 2020.

Conard, Edward. *The Upside of Inequality: How Good Intentions Undermine the Middle Class.* New York: Portfolio, 2016.

Cowen, Tyler. *The Complacent Class: The Self-Defeating Quest for the American Dream.* New York: St. Martin's Press, 2017.

Diamandis, Peter, and Steven Kotler. *The Future Is Faster Than You Think: How Converging Technologies Are Disrupting Business, Industries, and Our Lives.* New York: Simon & Schuster, 2020.

Diamond, Jared. *Collapse: How Societies Choose to Fail or Succeed.* New York: Penguin, 2004.

Diamond, Jared. *Upheaval: Turning Points for Nations in Crisis.* New York: Little, Brown, 2019.

Doudna, Jennifer, and Samuel Sternberg. *A Crack in Creation: Gene Editing and the Unthinkable Power to Control Evolution.* New York: Houghton Mifflin Harcourt, 2017.

Edwards, Sebastian. *The American Default: The Untold Story of FDR, the Supreme Court, and the Battle Over Gold.* Princeton, NJ: Princeton University Press, 2018.

Ferguson, Niall. *The Square and the Tower: Networks and Power, from the Freemasons to Facebook.* New York: Penguin, 2018.

Florida, Richard. *The New Urban Crisis: How Our Cities Are Increasing Inequality, Deepening Segregation, and Failing the Middle Class—and What to Do About It.* New York: Basic Books, 2017.

Fukuyama, Francis. *Identity: The Demand for Dignity and the Politics of Resentment.* New York: Farrar, Straus and Giroux, 2018.

Giridharadas, Anand. *Winners Take All: The Elite Charade of Changing the World.* New York: Knopf, 2018.

Goodwin, Doris Kearns. *Leadership: In Turbulent Times.* New York: Simon & Schuster, 2018.

Guillen, Mauro. *2030: How Today's Biggest Trends Will Collide and Reshape the Future of Everything.* New York: St. Martin's Press, 2020.

Howes, Anton. *Arts and Minds: How the Royal Society of Arts Changed a Nation.* Princeton, NJ: Princeton University Press, 2020.

Imbrie, Andrew. *Power on the Precipice: The Six Choices America Faces in a Turbulent World.* New Haven, CT: Yale University Press, 2020.

Joffe, Josef. *The Myth of America's Decline: Politics, Economics, and a Half Century of False Prophecies.* New York: Liveright, 2013.

Kälin, Christian. *Ius Doni: The Acquisition of Citizenship by Investment.* Zürich: Ideos Verlag, 2016.

Kissinger, Henry. *World Order.* New York: Penguin Press, 2014.

Klein, Ezra. *Why We're Polarized.* New York: Avid Reader Press/Simon & Schuster, 2020.

Klein, Matthew, and Michael Pettis. *Trade Wars Are Class Wars: How Rising Inequality Distorts the Global Economy and Threatens World Peace.* New Haven: Yale University Press, 2020.

Koehn, Nancy. *Forged in Crisis: The Making of Five Courageous Leaders.* New York: Scribner, 2017.

Kotkin, Joel. *The Coming of Neo-Feudalism: A Warning to the Global Middle Class.* New York: Encounter Books, 2020.

Krastev, Ivan. *Is It Tomorrow Yet? The Paradoxes of the Pandemic.* London: Allen Lane, 2020.

Kreitner, Richard. *Break It Up: Secession, Division, and the Secret History of America's Imperfect Union.* New York: Little, Brown, 2020.

Kristof, Nicholas, and Sheryl WuDunn. *Tightrope: Americans Reaching for Hope.* New York: Knopf, 2020.

Krznaric, Roman. *The Good Ancestor: A Radical Prescription for Long-Term Thinking.* New York: The Experiment, 2020.

Lewis, Michael. *The Fifth Risk: Undoing Democracy.* New York: W. W. Norton, 2018.

Lieven, Anatol. *Climate Change and the Nation State: The Case for Nationalism in a Warming World.* Oxford: Oxford University Press, 2020.

Lind, Michael. *The New Class War: Saving Democracy from the Managerial Elite.* New York: Portfolio/Penguin, 2020.

Lucas, Edward. *Spycraft Rebooted: How Technology Is Changing Espionage.* Amazon Publishing, 2018.

Luce, Edward. *The Retreat of Western Liberalism.* New York: Atlantic Monthly Press, 2017.

Mahbubani, Kishore. *Has China Won? The Chinese Challenge to American Primacy.* New York: PublicAffairs, 2020.

Markovits, Daniel. *The Meritocracy Trap: How America's Foundational Myth Feeds Inequality, Dismantles the Middle Class, and Devours the Elite.* New York: Penguin Press, 2019.

Micklethwait, John, and Adrian Wooldridge. *The Wake-Up Call: Why the Pandemic Has Exposed the Weaknesses of the West, and How to Fix It.* New York: HarperVia, 2020.

Naím, Moisés. *The End of Power: From Boardrooms to Battlefields and Churches to States, Why Being in Charge Isn't What It Used to Be.* New York: Basic Books, 2014.

Norberg, Johan. *Open: The Story of Human Progress.* New York: Atlantic Books, 2020.

Payne, Keith. *The Broken Ladder: How Inequality Affects the Way We Think, Live, and Die.* New York: Viking, 2017.

Piketty, Thomas. *Capital and Ideology.* Cambridge: Belknap Press/Harvard University Press, 2020.

Putnam, Robert B. *The Upswing: How Americans Came Together a Century Ago and How We Can Do It Again.* New York: Simon & Schuster, 2020.

Reeves, Richard. *Dream Hoarders: How the American Upper Middle Class Is Leaving Everyone Else in the Dust, Why That Is a Problem, and What to Do About It.* Washington, DC: Brookings Institution Press, 2017.

Roberts, Andrew. *Churchill: Walking with Destiny.* New York: Viking, 2018.

Rodrik, Dani. *Straight Talk on Trade: Ideas for a Sane Economy.* Princeton, NJ: Princeton University Press, 2017.

Rosen, William. *Justinian's Flea: The First Great Plague and the End of the Roman Empire.* London: Penguin Books, 2008.

Sandel, Michael. *The Tyranny of Merit: What's Become of the Common Good?* New York: Farrar, Straus and Giroux, 2020.

Scheidel, Walter. *The Great Leveler: Violence and the History of Inequality from the Stone Age to the Twenty-First Century.* Princeton, NJ: Princeton University Press, 2017.

Schroeter, John, ed. *After Shock: The World's Foremost Futurists Reflect on 50 Years of Future Shock—and Look Ahead to the Next 50.* Bainbridge Island, WA: John August Media, 2020.

Sitaraman, Ganesh. *The Great Democracy: How to Fix Our Politics, Unrig the Economy, and Unite America.* New York: Basic Books, 2019.

Sloane, Barney. *The Black Death in London*. Stroud, Gloucestershire: The History Press, 2011.

Stavridis, James. *Sailing True North: Ten Admirals and the Voyage of Character*. New York: Penguin, 2019.

Stavridis, James. *Sea Power: The History and Geopolitics of the World's Oceans*. New York: Penguin Press, 2017.

Strickler, Yancey. *This Could Be Our Future: A Manifesto for a More Generous World*. New York: Viking, 2019.

Thiel, Peter. *Zero to One: Notes on Startups, or How to Build the Future*. New York: Crown Business, 2014.

Vance, J. D. *Hillbilly Elegy: A Memoir of a Family and Culture in Crisis*. New York: Harper, 2016.

Wadhwa, Vivek, with Alex Salkever. *The Driver in the Driverless Car: How Our Technology Choices Will Create the Future*. Oakland: Berrett-Koehler, 2017.

Widmer, Ted. *Lincoln on the Verge: Thirteen Days to Washington*. New York: Simon & Schuster, 2020.

Yergin, Daniel. *The New Map: Energy, Climate, and the Clash of Nations*. New York: Penguin Press, 2020.

Zakaria, Fareed. *Ten Lessons for a Post-Pandemic World*. New York: W. W. Norton, 2020.

INDEX

ABOUT THE AUTHOR

"Paul Laudicina is one of the world's
foremost business strategists."
—MUHTAR KENT, *FORMER CHAIRMAN AND CEO,
THE COCA-COLA COMPANY; BOARD MEMBER,
3M AND SPECIAL OLYMPICS*

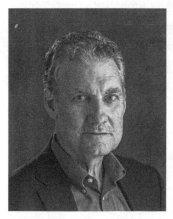

When Paul Laudicina arrived at the global management consulting firm Kearney, he brought with him a lifetime of experience—as a strategic planner for Mobil Oil Corporation, research associate at the United Nations, associate fellow at an economic policy think tank, legislative director for then–Senator Joseph R. Biden, and senior executive of SRI International (the former Stanford Research Institute), where he founded its policy division. His early life experience as a seminarian also helped form Paul's lifelong, principled, and passionate commitment to repairing what's broken or damaged.

And as he began his Kearney career, Paul saw a world grappling with sweeping political liberalization and rapidly accelerating globalization. So in 1991, he founded the Global Business Policy Council, a specialized strategic advisory services unit within Kearney, to help senior leaders in business, government, and civil society rise to the challenge of navigating in a transformed world. A quarter-century later, the Council is one of the world's best-known and most highly regarded private-sector think tanks.

Later, having become one of the firm's most respected and visible leaders, Paul was Kearney's first worldwide managing partner and chairman of the board to be elected following its 2006 management buyout, which returned the firm to partner ownership. During his six-year tenure, he guided Kearney through an extraordinary period of turnaround, renewal, and growth despite the Great Recession, expanding its global footprint to include offices in nearly 40 countries.

Throughout this extraordinary transformation, Paul has consistently been called upon for his leadership and vision—as founder and leader of the Council; as the firm's managing partner; as a trusted advisor and lead consultant to CEOs and boards of some of the world's largest companies; as a scenario planner and futurist; as a strategist advising governments and policymakers across the world; as a thought leader, author, columnist, commentator, and speaker; and as a mentor to a new generation of leaders. His achievements were recognized by his peers in 2019 with the consulting profession's highest distinction, the Lifetime Achievement Award, bestowed on Paul by *Consulting* magazine.

Paul is the author of many articles and several books, including *World Out of Balance: Navigating Global Risks to Seize Competitive Advantage* (McGraw-Hill, 2004) and *Beating the Global Odds: Successful Decision-Making in a Confused and Troubled World* (Wiley, 2012), which were both also published in numerous foreign language editions. He has been named multiple times to *Consulting* magazine's annual ranking of the Top 25 Most Influential Consultants.

A graduate of the University of Chicago in political science and government, he is the vice chancellor of the International Academy of

Management and a member of the Council on Foreign Relations. Paul is also a CEO Coach working with Korn Ferry, the world's largest executive search, human resources, and leadership development firm, through which he actively mentors a rising generation of CEOs.

Kearney, founded in 1926, is one of the pioneers of management consulting. However, it prides itself as being culturally quite distinct from its competitors—having always emphasized a practical, collegial, hands-on, and deeply collaborative way of working with clients. Today, with some 3,500 professionals (many with non-MBA backgrounds) working out of its global network of offices in over 40 countries, Kearney remains one of the most desirable places to work in the world. Its Global Business Policy Council, which Paul founded, is ranked as one of the world's top private-sector think tanks by the University of Pennsylvania in its most recent (and much-watched) comprehensive annual peer rankings of think tanks.

June 11, 2019

Dear Paul,

Congratulations on receiving *Consulting Magazine's* 2019 "Lifetime Achievement Award." I can't think of anyone more deserving of this noteworthy recognition.

Paul, I've had the distinct privilege of knowing you for most of your professional lifetime. This also makes me uniquely qualified to state without equivocation: You are a man of singular ability and character.

I remember, early in my Senate career, how impressed I was by the precocious 26-year-old who was working on national energy policy issues. Even back then, I saw that you had a special, omnivorous intellect. You have always had a remarkable ability to translate complicated policy questions into clear and compelling propositions that average Americans could understand. Yet you still always took the time to appreciate the merits of alternate points of view, finding ways to mediate them to improve the quality of any given policy.

But what I believe really distinguishes Paul Laudicina from the so many other bright and capable people I have worked with over the years, is your deep sense of decency and your sensitivity to the needs of struggling Americans. I know that your distinct sense of morality roots back to your family upbringing and your early days studying to become a priest. Your passion for being a positive force in life is apparent not only in the quality and nature of your professional achievements – but also in the lives that you've touched by going out of your way to offer a kind word or selfless action.

Paul, thank you agreeing to bring your unique expertise and unparalleled spirit to my Senate office. To this day, I feel immensely grateful for your brilliant service as my legislative director. I have trusted your counsel and called on you for advice more times than I can count – including after you left the Senate and while I was serving as Vice President. But even more significant than any piece of wisdom you've offered, I am the most grateful for your loyal and continued friendship.

The wonderful and well-earned honor you're receiving celebrates your lifetime of achievements that have positively impacted so many Americans. But don't let this award give you any ideas that somehow your work is finished. We need your talent, experience, and character now more than ever to address the great challenges ahead. I hope to see you soon, my friend.

Sincerely,

Joseph R. Biden, Jr.

Biden for President · P.O. Box 58174 · Philadelphia, PA 19102

PAID FOR BY BIDEN FOR PRESIDENT

Letter from then-presidential candidate Joe Biden read publicly on the occasion of Paul Laudicina's Lifetime Achievement Award ceremony in June 2019.